GENETICS

BREAKING THE CODE
OF YOUR DNA

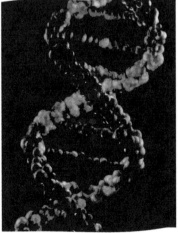

Carla Mooney
Illustrated by
Samuel Carbaugh

~ Titles in the *Inquire and Investigate* Series ~

green press INITIATIVE

Nomad Press is committed to preserving ancient forests and natural resources. We elected to print *Genetics: Breaking the Code of Your DNA* on Thor PCW containing 30% post consumer waste.

Nomad Press made this paper choice because our printer, Sheridan Books, is a member of Green Press Initiative, a nonprofit program dedicated to supporting authors, publishers, and suppliers in their efforts to reduce their use of fiber obtained from endangered forests.

For more information, visit www.greenpressinitiative.org.

This book was manufactured by Sheridan Books, Ann Arbor, MI USA.
April 2014, Job #357570
ISBN: 978-1-61930-208-2

Illustrations by Samuel Carbaugh
Educational Consultant, Marla Conn

Questions regarding the ordering of this book should be addressed to
Nomad Press
2456 Christian St.
White River Junction, VT 05001
www.nomadpress.net

Contents ▶

▾ TIMELINE

1859 .... Charles Darwin publishes *The Origin of Species*, which details his theory that populations evolve over generations through a process of natural selection. The work becomes the foundation of evolutionary biology.

1865 .... Gregor Mendel discovers "factors" or genes. He publishes the results of his experiments with pea plants. Mendel's work later becomes the foundation of the science of genetics.

1869 .... Swiss scientist Johann Friedrich Miescher isolates nuclein—later known as DNA.

1879 .... German scientist Walther Flemming sees chromosomes dividing inside a cell nucleus while looking at salamander larvae under a microscope.

1900 .... Three scientists—Carl Correns, Hugo de Vries, and Erich von Tschermak—independently discover and prove Mendel's principles. This marks the beginning of modern genetics.

1905 .... Nettie Stevens and Edmund Wilson independently describe the behavior of sex chromosomes, concluding that two X chromosomes create a female offspring, while an X and Y chromosome create a male offspring.

1910 .... Thomas Hunt Morgan proposes a theory that some traits are sex-linked. He bases this theory on a white-eye mutation discovered in fruit fly experiments.

1911 .... Thomas Hunt Morgan proves genes are carried on chromosomes.

1943 .... Oswald Avery discovers genes are made of DNA.

1953 .... James Watson and Francis Crick discover the double-helix structure of DNA.

1961 .... Sydney Brenner discovers messenger RNA.

1963 .... Chinese scientist Tong Dizhou removes DNA from a male carp and injects it into a cell from a female carp, making the first vertebrate animal clone.

▾ THE HISTORY OF GENETICS

1973 .... Stanley Cohen and Herbert Boyer clone genes by transferring a virus gene to bacteria.

1977 .... Fred Sanger and Walter Gilbert develop techniques to read and sequence chemical bases of DNA.

1983 .... Kary Mullis develops a copying machine to make copies of specific regions on DNA quickly in a test tube.

1983 .... The gene for Huntington's disease, a genetic disorder that affects muscle coordination and leads to cognitive and psychiatric problems, is located on chromosome 4.

1984 .... Alec Jeffreys develops DNA fingerprinting techniques that can be used to identify people and solve crimes.

1985 .... The gene for cystic fibrosis, a genetic disorder that often affects the lungs, is located on chromosome 7.

1988 .... The Human Genome Project begins with the goal of mapping the entire sequence of DNA in human chromosomes.

1990 .... Scientists propose to decode the human genome within 15 years.

1994 .... A genetically engineered tomato called the Flavr Savr is sold to the public for the first time. Production of the Flavr Savr tomato ends in 1997 because it was not profitable.

1998 .... Scientists use human embryonic stem cells to grow heart, blood, and bone cells.

2000 .... U.S. President Bill Clinton announces that scientists have completed a first draft of the human genome.

2005 .... The National Geographic Society and IBM launch a massive project to use DNA to map human migration during the last 60,000 years.

2013 .... In a clinical trial, doctors at the Children's Hospital of Philadelphia use gene therapy to treat children with leukemia.

Introduction▶
The Code of Life

Why do children look
like their parents?

Whether you have brown hair or blue eyes is determined by the genes that you received from your mom and dad.

Have you ever wondered why you have blond hair or brown eyes? Do you look like your mom or your dad? If you've asked these questions, you're not alone. Since the beginning of human history, people have wondered why they look the way they do. In fact, although children often look more like one parent than the other, most offspring appear to be a blend of the characteristics of both parents. This all leads to the question: How are traits inherited from one generation to the next?

It was early animal herders and farmers who first began to understand how traits are passed from one generation to the next. Herders noticed that if they used strong animals for breeding, the animals gave birth to strong, hearty offspring. Around the same time, early farmers used the same methods to improve crops. By planting only the best seeds, the farmers grew superior crops.

Over time, herders and farmers discovered general rules about inheritance. From experience, they found that some stable varieties of plants and animals bred true, which means their offspring had the same characteristics as the parents. Other types of animals and plants showed great variation in offspring. The herders and farmers also found that in some cases it was possible to create a hybrid from two different varieties, such as a mule, which is really half horse and half donkey. Occasionally, offspring were different from both parents, from a slight variation to a huge difference.

Although these early scientists understood some basic ideas about inheritance, they still did not have a scientific explanation for how traits were passed from parent to offspring. That explanation didn't come until 1865, when a monk named Gregor Mendel discovered that individual traits are determined by factors that are inherited from the parents. These factors would later be known as genes and would become the basic building blocks for the science of genetics.

WHAT IS GENETICS?

Genetics is the study of heredity. It's the branch of science that examines how traits are passed from one generation to the next. Genetics affects every living thing on Earth, from a tiny grass plant to a thundering elephant. The factors, or genes, that Gregor Mendel discovered are the fundamental units of heredity. Genes control how you look, behave, and reproduce. They pass from parent to child, from generation to generation.

There is a lot of new vocabulary in this book! Turn to the glossary in the back when you come to a word you don't understand. Practice your new vocabulary in the VOCAB LAB activities in each chapter.

SO, THESE TINY STRANDS OF INFORMATION ARE FOUND IN OUR CELLS?

Although genetics is a relatively young science, geneticists are scientists who work every day to learn more about genes and how they code for life. Some geneticists study how traits are inherited from parent to child. Others work to understand the chemical and physical structures of genes, determine how genes do their jobs, and identify which genes control which traits. All geneticists are trying to unlock the secrets of life!

THE CODE OF LIFE

The activities in *Genetics: Breaking the Code of Your DNA* will introduce you to the basic concepts of genetics that geneticists use to study genes and heredity. You will look inside a cell to study DNA, the genetic material, and how it codes for life. Along with genetics, this book will introduce you to related concepts in biology and chemistry. You will discover how geneticists use knowledge about genes to develop and support hypotheses about heredity. You will also learn how genetics is being used in several cutting-edge technologies, and the ethical questions that arise.

KEY IDEA

Use the QR codes throughout this book as takeoff points for further exploration. They suggest videos to view online and download. When a QR code is provided, you can use a smartphone or tablet app to access the suggestion directly.

Chapter 1 ▶
Gregor Mendel

How did Gregor
Mendel discover the
secrets of heredity?

How inheritance actually works remained a mystery until Gregor Mendel discovered genes, the foundation of heredity.

For centuries, scientists struggled to understand how traits were passed from parent to offspring. Farmers knew that breeding plants and animals with preferred physical traits often produced offspring that also had those valuable traits. But why was this so, and how did it happen?

THE FATHER OF GENETICS

GREGOR MENDEL: GREAT MINDS

Hear the dirt about Gregor Mendel and his pea plants. What scientific scandal about Mendel's data surfaced in the 1900s?

Gregor Mendel (1822–1884) was a monk who lived in a monastery in Brunn, Austria. As a child, Mendel had lived and worked on a farm. So in his spare time, Mendel bred pea plants in the monastery's gardens. He made careful observations of his plants, and noticed that the pea plants looked different from each other in several ways. Some plants were tall, others were short. Some had green seeds, others had yellow seeds. To discover what caused these differences, Mendel performed about 29,000 experiments.

MENDEL'S EXPERIMENT

Pea plants were well-suited to Mendel's experiments because they are easy to grow and they have many visible traits that can be followed from parent to offspring. Mendel investigated seven pea plant traits: the plant's height, seed shape, seed color, pod color, pod shape, color of the first leaves to grow (called cotyledons), and the flower position on the plant. Each trait had two forms that the plant could exhibit. For example, the plant's height could be either tall or short. Its seed shape could be either round or wrinkled.

Mendel started his experiment with true-breeding varieties of pea plants. These plants had shown only one of the two forms of the traits he was studying. These first plants were known as the parents or P1 generation. Mendel crossed each P1 parent plant with another P1 plant that had the opposite trait. For example, he crossed a tall plant with a short one and a plant from a round seed with a plant from a wrinkled seed.

Mendel controlled the pollination between his plants. To cross two plants, he removed the stamen from one and placed its pollen on the pistil of a different pea plant. He tied bags over the plants' flowers to prevent the wind or insects from carrying stray pollen to the plants.

After pollination, the flowers from the P1 generation plants produced seeds, which Mendel planted. The new plants that grew were called the F1 generation. Mendel allowed these plants to grow and self-pollinate, producing seeds that were a cross of two F1 plants. The plants that grew from these seeds were the F2 generation:

P1 **x** P1 ⟶ F1   F1 **x** F1 ⟶ F2

HOW PLANTS REPRODUCE

Plants use a dusty substance called pollen to reproduce. Pollen is produced by plant structures called stamen. Plant flowers also have structures called ovaries that are inside the flower's pistil. A flower's ovary produces eggs. When exposed to pollen during a process called pollination, the eggs are fertilized to produce seeds. If conditions are right, the seeds sprout into new plants and become the offspring of the plants that supplied the eggs and pollen. Pollination can happen when the pollen from one plant fertilizes the eggs of another plant. Other times, a plant's flower produces both eggs and pollen and self-fertilizes its own eggs.

The genes of an organism are its genotype. The way an organism looks is its phenotype. In Mendel's pea plants, two tall plants have the same phenotype, as they both look tall. The plants may have different genotypes, however. One plant may have two dominant alleles for tallness (TT), while the other plant may be a hybrid with a tall and a short allele for height (Tt). Alleles are different forms of the same gene. Short plants have both recessive alleles and the genotype tt. Organisms that have two of the same alleles (TT) are called homozygous, while organisms with two different alleles (Tt) are heterozygous.

WHEN I FIRST STARTED, I EXPECTED TO SEE A MIX OF TRAITS IN THE OFFSPRING.

For years, Mendel patiently moved pollen from plant to plant. He harvested and planted seeds. He carefully observed the results of each cross and recorded the number and traits of the offspring plants.

MENDEL'S RESULTS

The results of Mendel's pea plant experiments were extremely consistent. In every case, when he crossed two plants from the P1 generation, all of the F1 offspring had the same trait as one of the parent plants. For example, when he crossed a tall plant with a short plant, all of the offspring were tall. The result was surprising, because many people believed that inheritance was a blending of two traits. In other words, they expected a tall plant crossed with a short plant to produce a medium-sized plant.

When Mendel crossed two F1 offspring plants, he observed an interesting result. All of the F1 plants were tall, but their offspring were not. The short trait reappeared in about 25 percent of the F2 offspring. The remaining 75 percent were tall. Taking it one step further, Mendel discovered that when the F2 short offspring were crossed, they always produced short offspring. This result led him to conclude that the F2 short offspring were true breeders. In contrast, about one-third of the F2 tall offspring always produced tall offspring and were tall true breeders. The rest produced both tall and short offspring, in a ratio of 75 percent tall and 25 percent short.

Mendel discovered similar results for the other traits he crossed in his experiments. One trait appeared in all of the F1 generation plants. In the F2 generation, that same trait appeared three times more often than the other trait, in a ratio of 3:1.

MENDEL'S CONCLUSIONS

After thousands of crosses and observations, Mendel concluded that inheritance is not a blending of two traits, as many had believed. He concluded that the traits he was studying are controlled by factors that act in pairs. Today, we know these factors are genes. Offspring receive one gene from each parent to make a pair.

Mendel concluded that the factors that control traits can be dominant or recessive. A dominant trait masks the presence of a recessive trait. In Mendel's pea plants, round seed shape dominated wrinkled and green pods dominated yellow pods. When a plant received a dominant factor from one parent and a recessive factor from the other parent, the dominant factor was observed in the plant. So a plant that received a dominant tall factor and a recessive short factor from its parents grew tall.

Mendel reasoned that the factors that controlled the plants' traits were made of two distinct types, or alleles. For each offspring, the mother provides one allele, while the father provides the other allele. Those factors unite to form many possible combinations. In the offspring, both alleles can be dominant or recessive. The pair of alleles can also be a hybrid, with one allele dominant and the other recessive.

EXCEPTIONS TO THE RULE

Not all genes follow Mendel's laws of dominance. Some traits show incomplete dominance, where the two traits blend. For example, wavy hair is a mixture of the traits for straight and curly hair. It's lucky Mendel's plants followed his laws of dominance, otherwise he may never have figured out his laws of inheritance! Other traits show co-dominance, where both alleles are expressed. For example, the blood types A and B are both dominant. When a person inherits both of these alleles, a new blood type called AB is produced. Watch this clip to learn more about blood groups and the ideas of genetic dominance and co-dominance.

It is not possible to tell the genotype of a plant with a dominant phenotype from simply looking at it. Both heterozygous (Tt) and homozygous (TT) plants appear tall. Instead, scientists perform test crosses to determine the plant's genotype. If the plant only produces tall offspring, it is homozygous dominant. If it produces tall and short offspring, it is heterozygous dominant.

Mendel found that each of the seven traits he crossed were controlled by a single gene with two different alleles, one of which was dominant over the other. For example, the P1 pea plants crossed for height had two tall alleles (TT) or two short alleles (tt). Each parent gave one allele to the F1 offspring so that each offspring had a hybrid combination of alleles (Tt). Because the tall allele is dominant, it masked the short allele. This is why all of the F1 generation plants grew tall. When two F1 plants crossed, they could give either the tall allele (T) or the short allele (t) to their offspring. The table below, called a Punnett square, shows the possible combinations of alleles in the F2 generation:

Parent 1 - Tt	Parent 2 - Tt	
	T	**t**
T	TT	Tt
t	Tt	tt

This phenotype shows a 3:1 ratio—three of the plants will be tall (TT and Tt) and one will be short (tt). The genotype shows a 1:2:1 ratio—one contains only tall genes, two have one tall and one short, and one has two short genes. Mendel's law of segregation states that alleles for a trait separate randomly when male and female reproductive cells, called gametes, are formed. Each gamete, or sperm and egg, has an equal chance of receiving one of the alleles from each parent.

DOUBLE CROSS

Mendel also made crosses between plants with two different traits. For example, he crossed a tall plant with round seeds (TTSS) with a short plant with wrinkled seeds (ttss). Mendel wanted to find out if the genes for height and smoothness were linked or independent.

The F1 offspring displayed both dominant traits of tallness and smooth seeds. When Mendel crossed the F1 plants, he observed a ratio of 9:3:3:1 in the F2 offspring. Which traits did each plant display?

Parent 1 - TtSs	Parent 2 - TtSs			
	TS	Ts	tS	ts
TS	TTSS	TTSs	TtSS	TtSs
Ts	TTSs	TTss	TtSs	Ttss
tS	TtSS	TtSs	ttSS	ttSs
ts	TtSs	Ttss	ttSs	ttss

Now Mendel knew that the traits were independent. Whether a plant inherited a tall or short allele did not affect whether it inherited a smooth or wrinkled allele. This principle is called the law of independent assortment.

Although Mendel presented the results of his experiments in 1865, his work was largely ignored until the end of the century. At that time, three scientists working independently duplicated Mendel's experiments and results. Hugo de Vries, Erich von Tschermak, and Carl Correns discovered Mendel's work and announced his discovery to the world. Using Mendel's work as a basis, the study of genes and genetics ignited.

DOMINANT VS. RECESSIVE

Here are some examples of traits in humans that are dominant and recessive. Which do you have?

- Brown eyes are dominant over blue eyes.
- Brown hair is dominant over blond hair.
- Right-handedness is dominant over left-handedness.
- Unattached earlobes are dominant over attached earlobes.
- Color vision is dominant over color blindness.
- Extra fingers are dominant over five fingers.
- Double-jointedness is dominant over normal joints.
- Being able to curl your tongue is dominant over not being able to curl your tongue.

This video explains how Mendel's work helped scientists understand how traits are passed from parent to offspring.

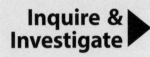

RECREATE MENDEL'S EXPERIMENT

Gregor Mendel used pea plants to study how certain traits were passed from parent to offspring. Using colored beads, you can recreate his experiment and develop a theory that explains the results of Mendel's experiment.

🧬 The scientific method is the way that scientists ask questions and find answers.

• **Start a scientific method worksheet to organize your questions and predictions.** What will happen when you cross tall pea plants with short pea plants? State your hypothesis. This is an unproven idea that tries to explain certain facts or observations.

• **The dark-colored beads represent the factor for tall pea plants and the light-colored beads represent the factor for short pea plants.** Place all of the dark beads in one paper cup, and all of the light beads in the other cup. Each cup represents a parent or P1 plant.

Scientific Method Worksheet
Questions: What are we trying to find out? What problem are we trying to solve?
Equipment: What did we use?
Methods: What did we do?
Predictions: What do we think will happen?
Results: What happened and why?

- **Mendel assumed that each plant passed one factor to its offspring.** Cross your two P1 plants to generate offspring by taking one bead from each cup and putting them together as an F1 generation offspring plant. Do this until you have several F1 offspring.

- **Examine the F1 offspring.** If the tall factor is dominant over the short factor, which trait will the F1 offspring exhibit? Try creating a simple Punnett square for the cross of the P1 generation. What inherited factors do the F1 plants have?

- **Now try crossing two F1 plants.** You can do this by mixing half of the dark beads and half of the light beads in one cup. Do the same for the second cup. Each cup represents a plant from the F1 generation. Without looking, select one bead from the first cup and one bead from the second cup. Together, the beads represent the factors passed to the F2 offspring plant. Record the results. Return the beads to their respective cups, shake the contents and draw a new combination. Record the results. Repeat this process at least 100 times.

- **Once you have created 100 crosses, you will have a good sample of what the F2 offspring will look like.** What are the different combinations of factors that the F2 plants can have? How many plants will be tall? How many will be short? Of those that are tall, how many are homozygous and how many are heterozygous? Create a chart that shows the frequency with which each combination of factors occurred. What is the ratio of your results? Does your data support Mendel's results? If not, why do you think this occurred?

WHAT ARE PUNNETT SQUARES

A Punnett square can be used to predict the outcome of a genetic cross. Check out this video that illustrates how scientists can use a Punnett square to predict a baby's hair color and whether or not the baby will have freckles.

To investigate more, design a Punnett square to model a cross of F2 plants. What different combinations of factors appear in the F3 offspring?

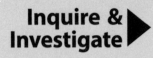
DOMINANT VS. RECESSIVE TRAITS

As Mendel discovered in his pea plant experiments, some human traits are controlled by dominant and recessive genes. Parents pass the genes that control these traits to their offspring. Which inherited traits do you have?

- **To track your results, create a table that will list the trait you are investigating and its possible phenotypes.** Each of the traits listed below has two phenotypes. You can start with these and add to your chart if there is something else you would like to investigate.

    a. Free earlobes vs. Attached earlobes

    b. Hair on fingers vs. No hair on fingers

    c. Widow's peak vs. No widow's peak

    d. Curly hair vs. Straight hair

    e. Cleft chin vs. Smooth chin

    f. Can roll tongue vs. Cannot roll tongue

🧬 Remember, the phenotype is the way an organism looks and the genotype is what genes it's made of.

Earlobes	Fingers	Hairline	Hair	Chin	Tongue
free	with hair	widow's peak	curly	cleft	can roll
attached	no hair	no widow's peak	straight	smooth	can't roll

Ideas for Supplies ▼
- paper
- pencil
- family members and friends to interview

- **Which of these traits do you have?** Record your answers on your table.

- **Survey the members of your family. What traits do they have?** Are they similar or different from yours? Do you see an inheritance pattern?

- **See if you find an inheritance pattern that extends farther into your extended family.** Choose one or two traits and survey some relatives outside your immediate family. Create a family tree that shows which phenotype each person has. Do you see an inheritance pattern? Can you make any predictions about what genotypes the different family members may have?

To investigate more, survey at least 20 people who are not related to you. Analyze your results. What traits are more common or dominant? What traits are less common? What percentage of people had each phenotype of a trait?

SWEET TOOTH

Love candy and cookies? Blame your parents! Researchers at Harvard Medical School and Mount Sinai School of Medicine discovered a sweet tooth gene in 2001. The gene is known as T1R3. It makes a protein that sends a signal to your brain when you've eaten a sugary food. People without the gene do not get that signal. Dr. Gopi Shaker of Mount Sinai, one of the scientists who studied the gene, says that if parents have a sweet tooth then it is likely their kids will too. However, there is evidence that behaviors can lessen the effect of the sweet tooth gene. By eating fewer sugary foods, you can diminish your craving for chocolate.

IS A SWEET TOOTH
A FAMILY TRAIT?

Some people have a sweet tooth, craving everything from jelly beans to chocolate, while others are not tempted by sugary treats. Can you blame your genes for your sweet tooth? Or is it a learned behavior? Try this experiment to find out!

- **Find as many family members as possible to interview and try to include at least three generations.** Brainstorm and write down the questions you want to ask to determine if someone has a sweet tooth and why. Be flexible and write down new questions you come up with during the interview. It's fun to find out right away if your interviewees think they have a sweet tooth or not. Then you can track how often people say they don't when they do, or they do when they don't!

- **Create a pedigree chart (see page 69 for instructions on how to make a pedigree chart) for the family members you interviewed.** Identify the people with a sweet tooth.

- **Analyze your pedigree chart to see if you can identify a pattern of inheritance.**

- **In the second phase of this experiment, you will test the sweet-tasting ability of the family members you interviewed.** Prepare several solutions of sugar water by dissolving sugar in water at three different ratios. Keep track of the ratios.

- **Pour small amounts of each solution into separate cups for family members to taste.** Come up with a system to keep track of what you are giving your family members without letting them know the concentration of the solution they are tasting.

- **Ask each family member to taste the three solutions and rate each on whether they could taste the dissolved sugar.** Did they like the more sugary ones or the less sugary ones? Record the results.

- **Compare the tasting results to whether or not the individual said he or she had a sweet tooth or not.** What do you find? What can you conclude from these results?

- paper and pencil
- several family members to interview
- paper cups
- water
- sugar
- measuring spoons or cups

To investigate more, expand your survey to several additional families and create separate pedigree charts and surveys for each. Are your results consistent from family to family?

INHERITANCE OF TWO INDEPENDENT TRAITS

As Mendel conducted his pea plant experiments, he wondered if the traits he observed were linked or independent. What would happen if he crossed pea plants that had two pairs of distinct traits? You can use everyday objects to simulate a cross of pea plants with two traits: tall vs. short and smooth vs. wrinkled seeds.

🧬 Mendel concluded that the traits he was studying were controlled by factors that acted in pairs. These factors could be dominant or recessive. A dominant trait masks the presence of a recessive trait.

- **Start a scientific method worksheet to organize your questions and predictions.** How can you use different colored beads and paper clips to represent different traits? Will the traits behave as separate factors? Or will they pass from parent to offspring together? State your hypothesis.

🔬 VOCAB LAB

Write down what you think each word means: **genes, alleles, phenotype, genotype, homozygous, heterozygous, dominant**, and **recessive**. Discuss your definitions with friends using real life examples. Did you all come up with the same definitions? Turn to the text and the glossary if you need help.

- **Set up your experiment to cross two parents with two independent traits.** What does each type of bead and paper clip represent? Place the beads and paper clips into the cups to create the F1 generation parents in your experiment. How did you divide the beads and clips? How did you pair the cups? Does each parent have traits for height and smoothness?

- **Simulate a genetic cross and create F2 generation offspring.** Gently shake the cups to mix up the contents. Select beads and clips from each F1 parent to create your offspring. How many alleles does each offspring have?

- **Create a table to record the results of your cross.** Write down the offspring's factors, genotype, and phenotype. Return the beads and paper clips to their original cups.

- **Keep drawing beads and paper clips to form new F2 offspring and record the results until you have the traits for 100 different offspring.** Make sure to record the genotype and phenotype of each.

- **Analyze your results.** How accurate were your predictions? Make a chart to show the results visually. What genotype was most common? What was least common? What phenotype was most common and what was least common? How do your results compare to Mendel's finding of a 9:3:3:1 phenotype ratio?

Ideas for Supplies ▼

- paper
- pencil
- dark-colored beads and light-colored beads, 48 of each
- dark-colored paper clips and light-colored paper clips, 48 of each
- 4 paper cups

To investigate more, design a model to simulate crossing two F2 plants to generate F3 offspring. What phenotypes and genotypes do you observe in the F3 generation? What is the ratio of phenotypes that you observe?

Ideas for Supplies ▼

- family members to survey and fingerprint
- pencil and paper
- wet paper towels
- black ink pad
- white printer paper
- magnifying glass

To investigate more, fingerprint and analyze several more families. How do their results compare with your family? Are the results consistent? What can you conclude from your results?

ARE FINGERPRINTS INHERITED?

Like DNA, fingerprints are unique to every person and they come in three basic shapes: loops, whorls, and arches. Do you think the basic shapes run in families? In this experiment, you'll investigate whether or not fingerprints are an inherited trait.

- **Create a chart to track your results.** What information are you going to need to include?

- **Make sure each subject's index finger is clean.** One at a time, roll the subject's index finger on the inkpad and gently roll it from one side to the other on a piece of white paper. Keep track of which family member you are printing. Can you identify each print as a loop, whorl, or arch?

- **When you've completed each family member, analyze your chart for an inheritance pattern.** What do you notice?

Chapter 2▶ Looking Inside the Cell

I'M KIND OF A BIG, LITTLE, DEAL!

Why are the cells important to genetics?

DX Cells are like tiny suitcases that carry all of your genetic material. The cells contain special structures that allow them to pass your genes on to new cells—and to your children.

Although Gregor Mendel never saw a gene with his own eyes, he believed that something inside an organism controlled heredity. Today we know that all living things are made of cells. Cells are small compartments that hold all of the biological equipment and information necessary for an organism to grow and stay alive. Within a single organism, there may be many types of cells. In humans, there are hundreds of types of cells. Some cells carry oxygen, while others form muscle or skin tissue.

Understanding how cells work is an important part of studying genetics. Genetic material is found in an organism's cells and is passed from one generation to the next through the cell's process of growing and dividing. Understanding how cells work is the foundation for understanding how genetics works.

INSIDE THE CELL

As microscopes became more powerful, scientists were able to look inside cells and see their internal structure. What they saw resembled a plastic bag with a few tiny holes surrounding every cell. We now know this is the cell membrane, which holds all of the cell structures and fluid inside the cell and blocks unwanted materials from entering the cell. The tiny holes allow some objects to move in and out of the cell. Inside the cell membrane, several organelles float within the cell's jellylike cytoplasm. Two of the most important organelles are mitochondria and chloroplasts.

Mitochondria, the "powerhouse of the cells," generate more than 90 percent of the energy needed by the body to sustain life and support growth. Its primary role is to extract energy from nutrients such as fat, protein, and glucose to produce adenosine triphosphate (ATP). Cells store ATP until they need it for energy. Animals and plants have mitochondria. In plants, chloroplasts process the sun's energy into sugars that the plant's mitochondria can use to generate energy.

Another look inside the cell membrane reveals a spherical object that is protected by its own membrane. That object is called the nucleus, the command center of the cell. The nucleus holds long, string-like segments of genetic material known as chromosomes (which we'll explore further in Chapter 4). The double-layered nuclear membrane surrounding the nucleus protects the chromosomes from damage. Tiny pores allow proteins to pass through while keeping the chromosomes safely inside.

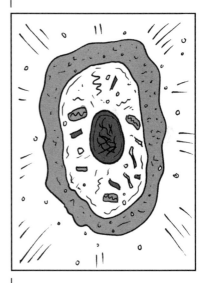

Organisms constantly produce new cells. Sometimes new cells are needed for growth, while other times they replace older cells that have become worn out or damaged.

Some cells, such as in the heart, eyes, and brain, stay in interphase all their lives without ever copying their DNA. This means if these cells are damaged, they can never be replaced.

CELL CYCLE

Most eukaryotic cells (cells with a nucleus) follow a pattern of growth and division called the cell cycle. In the cycle, the cell goes through growth phases, nuclear division or mitosis, and cytokinesis.

The longest stage of a cell's life cycle is spent in interphase. This is the growth stage between one cell division and the next. Interphase has three segments: G1 (first gap), S (synthesis), and G2 (second gap). G1 is when the cell carries out most of its normal functions of growth and protein production. In the S phase, DNA in the cell's nucleus replicates and creates two copies of each chromosome. During G2, the cell grows, duplicating its organelles, in preparation for mitosis and cell division.

MAKING NEW CELLS WITH MITOSIS

To create new cells, an existing cell undergoes a process of cell division called mitosis. During interphase, the cell prepares itself for mitosis, and its chromosomes replicate in the nucleus (or in the cytoplasm if the cell doesn't have a nucleus). Each copy is a loosely bundled coil called a chromatid, and the duplicate chromosomes, known as sister chromatids, carry the exact same genetic material.

Mitosis occurs in four stages: prophase, metaphase, anaphase, and telophase. During prophase, the DNA of each sister chromatid becomes very compact, making them visible under a microscope. The copies link together as a unit and join at a point called the centromere.

In metaphase, the nuclear membrane dissolves and the chromosomes can move freely across the cell. The double-stranded chromosomes line up across the center of the cell. Threadlike strands called spindles grab each sister chromatid around its centromere. The spindles are attached to points on either side of the cell called poles. If you imagine a globe, the chromosomes would be lined up at the equator and attached to the poles at either end of the globe.

In anaphase, the spindle fibers pull the sister chromatids apart. Every pair is split so that a full set of the original cell's chromosomes is pulled to each end of the cell. During telophase, a new nuclear membrane forms around each set of chromosomes. The chromosomes unwind and transition into G1 to prepare for the next cell division. At the end of telophase, the cytoplasm of the cell pinches itself in half and divides into two smaller, yet identical daughter cells in a process called cytokinesis.

The process of mitosis ensures that every new cell has a perfect and complete set of chromosomes that are identical to the original parent cell. In addition, all of the cell organelles and cytoplasm are divided between the two new daughter cells. The new cells are ready to start the cell division cycle again.

WALTHER FLEMMING

In 1879, Walther Flemming was the first scientist to describe how chromosomes moved during mitosis. Flemming studied cell division in salamander embryos. He stained the chromosomes to see them clearly. Some of the names Flemming used for the phases of cell division, such as prophase, metaphase, and anaphase, are still used today.

Are you ready to see the steps in mitosis for yourself?

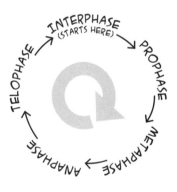

INTERPHASE (STARTS HERE)
PROPHASE
METAPHASE
ANAPHASE
TELOPHASE

Check out these links.

WHEN A CELL GOES THROUGH MITOSIS, THINK OF THE BRAIN OF THE CELL COPYING ITSELF...

...AND TAKING HALF OF ITS GUTS WITH EACH NEW CELL. THEY WOULD GROW NEW GUTS.

AND IT'S HAPPENING IN YOU RIGHT NOW!

CREATE A MITOSIS MODEL

Cells reproduce themselves by dividing during mitosis. The DNA in the cell's nucleus replicates, resulting in two copies of each chromosome. The double chromosomes separate and are pulled to opposite sides of the cell. A second process called cytokinesis pinches off the cell's membrane to form two new cells. Both new cells contain an exact copy of the original parent cell's chromosomes.

Organisms use mitosis to grow and to replace cells that are worn out or damaged. This model will show how chromosomes are copied during mitosis.

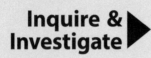 **Mitosis is the process of cell division that creates new, identical cells. The four stages of mitosis are prophase, metaphase, anaphase, and telophase.**

- **On a piece of paper, draw a large shape to represent a cell with a vertical line dividing it in half.** What shape should you choose?

Ideas for Supplies ▼

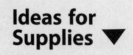

- pencil
- paper
- pipe cleaners
- scissors
- marker

- **Use pipe cleaners to create several pairs of chromosomes. How many pipe cleaners will you need?** How will you arrange them? How will you tell them apart?

- **Create a second set of chromosomes that are identical to the ones that you already made.** What do these represent? Where do you find them in the cell during this phase of mitosis? How should the two copies interact?

- **Line up the chromosomes in your cell as you would expect them to prepare for mitosis.** Are they along the middle line, at the poles, or floating around?

- **Pull all of the chromosomes on one side of the vertical line toward the cell's pole.** Where do the remaining chromosomes move? What does the cell look like now?

- **Draw two new circles around the two groups of chromosomes to represent the two new daughter cells.** How does each daughter cell compare to the original parent cell?

> To investigate more, repeat the process of mitosis using the two daughter cells. What does the next generation of cells look like? How are their chromosomes the same or different?

OK, SO NOW HOW DO WE SORT THE PIPE CHROMOSOMES?

BY NAME! THIS ONE IS TED.

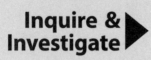
EXTRACT YOUR OWN DNA

DNA is located inside the nucleus of most cells. This large molecule carries all the genetic information in a cell, so you could say that DNA holds the instruction manual for life. It codes for all of an organism's characteristics. Each DNA molecule is a long, thin thread. In this experiment, you will collect some cells from inside your mouth and isolate the DNA.

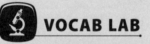
- **Set things up by mixing a salt solution and a soap solution.** For the salt solution, pour about 10 milliliters of distilled water into a paper cup. Add about 1 gram of salt and stir. For the soap solution, pour about 3 milliliters of distilled water into the other paper cup. Add about 1 milliliter of liquid soap and stir.

- **Swish the salt water in your mouth for 30 seconds—but do not swallow it.** After you finish swishing, spit it back into the paper cup. What are some different cells that might be in your mouth? What do you think is in the salt water now?

- **Pour the salt water into the test tube, not quite half full.** Add about 1 milliliter of the soap solution into the test tube. How can you gently mix the contents without other kinds of cells getting into the test tube? What other cells might get in there?

- **Pour some chilled ethyl alcohol into the test tube to almost fill it, but do not stir or mix.** Does the alcohol sink to the bottom or stay on top of the soap solution? Why do you think this happens?

- **Wait two minutes, then examine the contents of the test tube.** What do you see? What does it look like and what makes it clump together? If you want to keep your DNA, use a wooden stick or a straw to collect the strands and transfer them to a small container filled with alcohol.

> To investigate more, try using different soaps and detergents. How do powdered soaps work compared to liquid detergents? What about shampoo or liquid body soap? Can you think of any other sources of DNA to experiment with? Do you need to prepare the solutions in a different way to see the DNA?

Ideas for Supplies ▼

- distilled water
- paper cups
- salt
- liquid dishwashing soap
- 95-percent ethyl alcohol, chilled
- graduated cylinder with milliliter markings
- test tube
- wooden stick or straw
- plastic wrap

BLAH! SOMETIMES SCIENCE TASTES BAD...

Chapter 3 ▶
DNA:
The Genetic Material

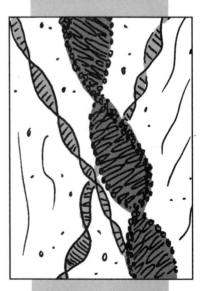

What is the job of
DNA in the cell?

🧬 Your genes are made of DNA, which carries the instructions for making a cell's proteins These proteins determine your characteristics and enable you to live and grow.

Inside the cell nucleus, a macromolecule called deoxyribonucleic acid (DNA) carries the organism's genetic information. Every living thing on Earth, from the smallest insect to the largest elephant has DNA that stores its genetic information. DNA is like an instruction manual, holding information that an organism needs to grow and function. Segments of DNA called genes code the instructions to make specific proteins and control a cell's activities. DNA is essential for every living thing!

DISCOVERING DNA

When Mendel was experimenting with pea plants in the 1860s, no one knew about DNA. Mendel was on the right track when he concluded that factors, or genes, from parents controlled traits in their offspring. What he didn't know was that these factors were actually contained in an organism's DNA.

For decades, many scientists worked to find life's genetic material, contributing pieces of knowledge that would eventually lead to our understanding of DNA. In 1928, Fred Griffith studied the pneumococcus bacteria, which causes pneumonia in people and kills mice. He injected one strain into mice and the mice died. He injected another strain into mice and the mice lived. He then heated up the first strain to kill the disease, injected it into the mice, and the mice lived. But when he mixed the heated strain with the other strain, the mice still died. Something in the heated strain transformed the strain that didn't kill mice into a strain that did kill them. This became known as the transforming principle.

Following on Griffith's work, by the mid-twentieth century, most scientists believed that a macromolecule called DNA was responsible for the transfer of genetic information. But they still didn't know what DNA looked like or how it worked.

In 1949, Austrian scientist Erwin Chargaff studied DNA from many organisms. He discovered that they all had something in common. Every DNA molecule had four types of nitrogen bases: adenine, cytosine, guanine, and thymine. Chargaff had discovered a significant clue about DNA, but he was unable to figure out its structure.

In the early 1950s, English scientists Rosalind Franklin and Maurice Wilkins worked at King's College in London to find DNA's structure. They tried to see what DNA looked like by bouncing X-rays off the molecule. The technique created a shadow picture of the molecule's structure showing rungs like those on a ladder between two side-by-side strands that cross in a spiral helix shape.

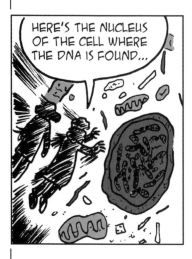

Around the same time, American molecular biologist James Watson and British molecular biologist Francis Crick were also working to understand DNA's structure by building models of DNA using sticks and balls. In 1953, Wilkins secretly showed some of Franklin's findings to Watson. Combining this information with Chargaff's studies, Watson and Crick realized that the DNA molecule was made of two chains of nucleotides that were paired to form a double helix.

Using scale-model atoms, they observed that the base adenine fit together with thymine, while guanine fit with cytosine like jigsaw pieces. They realized that if these bases always paired together, it would explain why the bases always occurred in equal numbers. Eureka! Watson and Crick had cracked the mystery of DNA. For their work, Watson, Crick, and Wilkins received the Nobel Prize in Medicine in 1962.

DNA'S DOUBLE HELIX

Watson and Crick discovered that the DNA macromolecule is made of two strands that are twisted in the shape of a double helix. If you were to untwist the double helix and lay it flat, it would look like a ladder. Each side of the ladder is a DNA strand that is made of thousands of units called nucleotides.

A DNA nucleotide has three parts: a sugar called deoxyribose, a phosphate group, and a nitrogenous base. The sugar is linked to the phosphate group on one end and a base at the other end. Picturing the DNA structure as a ladder, the two sides are strands of sugar and phosphate, while the bases extend out and link together by hydrogen bonds to form the ladder's rungs.

The base adenine (A) always pairs with thymine (T) and guanine (G) always pairs with cytosine (C). Therefore, in every DNA molecule the amount of one base is equal to the amount of its complementary base. Because all four bases are flat molecules, they stack up tightly, like a pile of coins. This tight stacking makes the DNA molecule compact and strong.

Inside a cell, the twisted double-helix shape of DNA serves two purposes. First, it makes DNA easy to replicate for cell division and making proteins. The double helix shape also protects the bases on the inside of the helix and prevents damage to the information in DNA.

The order of the four DNA bases forms DNA's code. The sequence of the bases forms the language that tells the cell what to do. Although there are only four different bases, they can form in endless sequences. Even though a complete strand of DNA can be millions of base pairs long, it would take nearly 5,000 strands of DNA laid side by side to equal the width of a human hair. The sequence and length of DNA's base pairs is what makes each of us unique. In fact, no two organisms, except for identical twins, have the same sequence of bases in their DNA.

DNA's ladder is made of thousands of units called nucleotides. A nucleotide has three parts: a deoxyribose sugar, a phosphate group, and a nitrogenous base. Every DNA molecule has four nitrogen bases: adenine, cytosine, guanine, and thymine. Adenine always pairs with thymine, while cytosine always pairs with guanine. The order of the four bases forms DNA's code, which carries the instructions for making a cell's proteins.

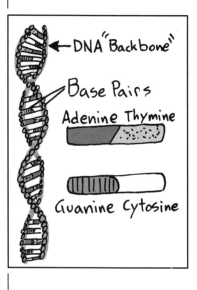

CATCHING MISTAKES

Although mistakes can happen during DNA replication, they are rare. To catch errors, an enzyme called DNA polymerase checks the pairing of new bases through a process called proofreading. This process works in much same way you might proofread a test before turning it in to the teacher. If the wrong base is in place, the bond on the ladder rung is unstable. When the DNA polymerase finds a mistake or a missing base, it cuts out the incorrect base and replaces it with the correct one. DNA proofreading eliminates most of the mistakes made in replication.

DNA REPLICATION

DNA carries the instructions for making a cell's proteins. These proteins determine an organism's characteristics and enable the living organism to function. When the cell reproduces, it passes these instructions to the new cells.

Before a cell can reproduce, it replicates its DNA. If the organism is a eukaryote with cells having a nucleus, DNA replication occurs in the nucleus. If it's a prokaryote, DNA replication takes place in the cell's cytoplasm. Either way, the basic process is the same. The double helix structure breaks apart down the middle to form two strands. Each side then serves as a pattern to assemble the other side.

During the interphase of the cell cycle, right before mitosis begins, special enzymes move along the DNA ladder to unzip the molecule, working in small sections. As the strand is unzipped, several small proteins called single-strand binding proteins temporarily bind to each side of the helix and keep them separated. Then new nucleotides move into each side of the unzipped ladder and pair with their complementary nucleotides on each strand. Bases that are not complementary bounce away from each other. In this way, the old strand of DNA directs the creation of the new strand. Another enzyme seals the bases together from the old and new strands, reforming DNA's double helix.

When the replication process is complete, the cell has two identical molecules of DNA. Each molecule contains one side of the original DNA and one side created with new nucleotides. The new copies automatically wind up again and the cell division process begins.

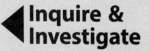

MAKE A 3D MODEL
OF THE DNA DOUBLE HELIX

The genetic information for each organism is held in DNA, a macromolecule found in the nucleus of almost every cell. DNA is made up of two strands created by thousands of nucleotides that are twisted in the shape of a double helix. In this project, you will build and analyze the structure of the DNA ladder.

Ideas for Supplies ▼

- red and black hollow licorice sticks
- scissors
- string
- jelly beans (at least four different colors)
- small marshmallows
- toothpicks

- **Cut the red and black licorice sticks lengthwise.** Use the licorice and string to create two sides of the DNA ladder. What does each color represent? What pattern did you create for the ladder sides?

- **Sort the jelly beans to represent the four different bases.** Which colors will pair with each other as you build your ladder? Why?

- **Using marshmallows as hydrogen bonds and the jelly beans as bases, build the rungs of your DNA ladder with toothpicks.** What does each rung look like? What patterns do you see?

- **Attach the ladder rungs to the licorice sides of your ladder.** Where do you attach the rungs? After you have built the ladder, what do you need to do to complete your model of a DNA double helix?

To investigate more, compare your DNA ladder to your classmates' ladders. How are they similar? How are they different?

THE HARDEST PART ABOUT THIS IS NOT EATING THE LICORICE DNA.

DNA REPLICATION

Almost every cell has an identical copy of an organism's DNA. To create new cells with the same instructions, the DNA replicates itself. DNA's double helix structure is very useful for replication. The double helix breaks apart down the middle to form two strands of DNA. The bases on each side serve as the pattern to reform the other side of the ladder. In this experiment, you will break apart a DNA model and replicate it.

VOCAB LAB

Write down what you think each word means: **macromolecule, deoxyribonucleic acid (DNA), nucleotide, enzyme, nitrogen base,** and **proofread.** Discuss your definitions with friends. Did you all come up with the same definitions? Turn to the text and the glossary if you need help.

Ideas for Supplies ▼

- construction paper in seven different colors
- scissors
- tape or stapler

- **Cut the construction paper into several strips approximately 1 inch across and 6 inches long.** Repeat for each color of paper.

- **Using the construction paper strips, create rings and link them together to form a DNA ladder.** What does each color represent? Where are the sugars, the phosphate groups, the four bases, and the hydrogen bonds in your DNA ladder?

- **Now that you have created a DNA model, simulate replication.** What is the first step in replication? What does your model look like after you complete this step?

- **Using the separate ladder sides and bases, recreate the DNA ladder's missing side and rungs. How do you attach the bases to the new side?** How do you know what sequence of bases to use as you replicate the DNA? Repeat until all the missing pieces are replaced. You've replicated your DNA!

To investigate more, lay the two complete DNA ladders next to each other and carefully compare each. Are the ladders identical? If not, why not?

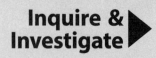
EXTRACT DNA FROM FRUIT

All living organisms have DNA, including the fruit you eat. DNA holds the blueprint that directs the building of living things. Every cell in an organism holds its DNA. In this experiment, you will use a few simple items to extract DNA from a piece of fruit.

EXTRACTED DNA— NOW WHAT?

Once DNA is extracted, scientists can examine it to discover more information about the person, animal, or plant from which it came. At a crime lab, forensic scientists compare DNA samples to samples taken from the crime scene and suspects. If the two samples match, the investigators know that the suspect was present at the crime scene. Scientists also examine extracted DNA to look for signs of genetic defects or to figure out if two people are related to each other. Scientists can even determine if a plant has been altered in any way, perhaps with specific genes to make it bigger or disease-resistant.

- **Create a solution of shampoo and water.** You only need a couple of spoonfuls of shampoo. Use twice as much water as shampoo, then add two to three pinches of salt.

- **In a separate cup, mash the fruit and add in a little water to the fruit pulp.** Why do you need to mash the fruit? How do you think it might help extract the DNA?

- **How much water did you add to the shampoo?** This is the amount of fruit pulp-water mixture you should add to the shampoo-water-salt mixture. Gently mix until it is a uniform consistency. What role does the shampoo play in your solution? What role does the salt play?

- **Place the coffee filter in another cup, then carefully pour all of the shampoo-fruit mixture into the filter.** Why do you need to filter your mixture? What does the liquid in the cup look like?

- **Pour some alcohol into a small glass or test tube.** Using the eyedropper, take the filtered fruit liquid and slowly drop it into the alcohol. Do not shake this mixture. What do you see? What does it look like? How does the alcohol act on the DNA?

> To investigate more, repeat this experiment with another type of fruit. How is the experiment's result different? How is it the same?

...JUST NOT A SMOOTHIE ONE SHOULD EVER DRINK.

Chapter 4 ▶
Genes and Chromosomes

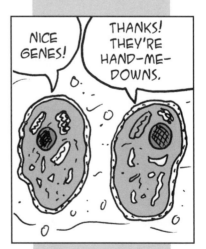

What is the difference
between genes
and chromosomes
and how are they
organized in the cell?

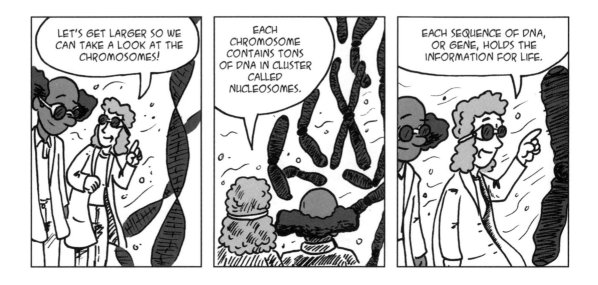

 Every living thing has a certain number of paired chromosomes that contain sections of DNA called genes. Each chromosome can contain hundreds or even thousands of genes.

CONFUSED ABOUT GENES?

Try this short video to learn more about genes, what they look like, what they do, and the idea behind genetically modified organisms.

Every cell in your body holds an impressively large amount of DNA in a tiny space. The DNA from a single human cell would stretch out three meters long, about as long as a car! We each have enough DNA to reach to the sun and back more than 300 times or around the equator more than 2 million times. If you've got long hair, you know it can be almost impossible to keep it from tangling. So what keeps extremely long DNA strands from getting hopelessly entwined? Chromosomes!

Inside the cell, DNA does not float around randomly. To fit inside the nucleus, DNA has to package itself down to less than one 10,000th of its original length. This happens in a couple of stages.

First, the long DNA strands neatly wind around proteins in the nucleus called histones, like thread around a spool. Each of these wrapped bundles is called a nucleosome. A chain of nucleosomes makes a chromatin and is often described as looking like "beads on a string."

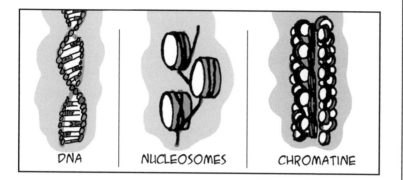

DNA | NUCLEOSOMES | CHROMATINE

As the cell prepares for mitosis, the chromatin gets more and more organized to take up less and less space. It becomes shorter and thicker, eventually forming a chromosome made of the pairs of tightly bound chromatids that later pull apart and unwind to start the process once again.

Every organism has a specific number of chromosomes in each cell. And this number has nothing to do with the size of the organism. Mosquitoes have six chromosomes, while carp have 104 chromosomes. In a human cell, there are 46 chromosomes. They come in 23 pairs, one complete set from your mom and the other from your dad. Of the 23 pairs, 22 are autosomal chromosomes, which are identified by numbers 1 through 22. The remaining pair is made of the sex chromosomes, which determine the gender of the offspring.

Most of the time, chromosomes are loose and string-like in their chromatin form. When the cell is about to divide, they thicken and shorten. Using high-powered microscopes and a staining technique, scientists are able to see chromosomes when they thicken. Stained chromosomes look like striped tubes pinched in the center. Each end of a chromosome is capped by a telomere, which is made of densely packed DNA. The telomere is designed to protect the chromosome's DNA instructions.

THE FLY ROOM

Between 1910 and 1930, scientist Thomas Hunt Morgan and his students at Columbia University studied fruit flies and heredity in a lab nicknamed the Fly Room. Their research made several contributions to genetics. Working with thousands of flies, Morgan and his colleagues confirmed the chromosomal theory of inheritance, which states that genes are located on chromosomes. They also found that some genes located close together on a string of DNA are linked, which means they are on the same chromosome and are always passed to offspring together. Would Mendel have been able to figure out his law of independent assortment if the genes for the traits he followed were linked? One of Morgan's students, Alfred Sturtevant, created the first genetic map, also known as a linkage map. In 1933, Morgan received the Nobel Prize for his work on the chromosome theory of inheritance.

🧬 Each pair of chromosomes has similar genes, although they may not be identical. Some physical traits are controlled by a single gene, while others are controlled by multiple genes. Gene regulation determines which genes the cell needs to use and when to turn them on.

If you compare pictures of chromosomes, you'll notice subtle differences between each one. Scientists use size, banding pattern, and centromere position to identify each chromosome and distinguish it from another. On any chromosome, the centromere might be in the middle, or closer to the top or bottom, making the chromosome appear as if it has two segments or arms of unequal lengths. In addition, each chromosome has a unique striping, or banding pattern. These bands divide a chromosome into regions and are used to identify different sections of a chromosome.

Scientists sort chromosomes into matching pairs using a picture called a karyotype. First, they take pictures of a person's chromosomes through a microscope. Then they rearrange the chromosomes by size, from largest to smallest, each paired with its match. Once the karyotype is complete, a trained geneticist can examine it for abnormalities.

WHAT ARE GENES?

Chromosomes contain sections of DNA called genes. Genes tell the body how, when, and where to make the structures that are necessary for life. Genes hold instructions for making proteins in the cell that make the body function. Cell proteins are responsible for the color of your eyes, the color of your hair, and the size of your feet. On a single chromosome, there can be hundreds or thousands of genes. Scientists believe that humans have about 20,000 to 25,000 genes.

Each pair of chromosomes has two copies of the same genes. You inherit one copy of a gene on the chromosome from your mother and the other copy on the chromosome from your father. While the two genes are similar, they are not necessarily identical. For example, both genes may control how your earlobes are shaped. One may have the gene for attached earlobes, while the other has the gene for free earlobes. Different versions of a gene are its alleles. Any gene can have one or more alleles.

Some physical traits are controlled by a single pair of genes, such as a widow's peak or attached earlobes. Many traits, however, are controlled by multiple genes. For these traits, several genes act together to produce the phenotype you see. The genes may be located at different points on the same chromosome or on different chromosomes.

Without genes, the body could not make the proteins it needs for life. Cells use the protein-building instructions coded into genes every time they need to build a protein. For example, red blood cells transport oxygen throughout the body. The cells use a protein called hemoglobin to carry the oxygen. Genes tell the cell how to build hemoglobin. If there is a problem with the gene, the body may not be able to make hemoglobin properly. This can lead to a serious genetic disorder known as sickle cell anemia, which affects the shape of red blood cells.

GENE REGULATION

JUMPING GENES

In 1944, Barbara McClintock discovered that genes were not fixed on chromosomes as scientists had previously thought. Studying corn, McClintock found that certain genes could jump around on chromosomes without a piece of a chromosome having broken off and attaching to another chromosome. Later, jumping genes were found in many organisms, from bacteria to humans. McClintock won the Nobel Prize in 1983 for her work.

Every cell has a complete copy of an organism's DNA, which is like having access to an entire library of information. Yet each cell has a specific job. Blood cells may make hemoglobin proteins, while skin cells do not. Therefore, a cell only uses the information in the DNA library that holds the instructions for its job, like checking out only a few books from the library. So how does a cell decide which genes to check out or turn on?

Gene regulation determines which genes the cell needs to use and when to turn them on. A skin cell will turn on the genes that make skin. On the other hand, a blood cell would leave those genes turned off, because the instructions for making skin aren't part of its job. Genes turn on when they are needed, and turn off like a light switch when they are not. Genes turn on as a response to several stimuli. Some genes turn on in response to cues from the cells around them. Others are triggered by external environmental influences such as heat and light. Still others turn on and turn off at certain points in an organism's development.

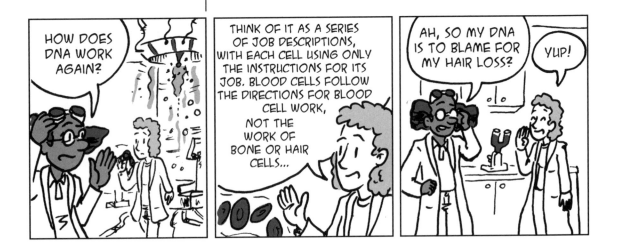

THE GENOME AND THE HUMAN GENOME PROJECT

Together, a full set of an organism's chromosomes is its genome. The size of a genome is usually measured by the number of nucleotide base pairs of A-T and C-G it contains. Scientists believe the human genome contains about 3 billion pairs.

An organism's genome contains all of the information it needs for life. The challenge is that a genome is written in the strange language of DNA. To understand the instructions, you first have to figure out how to read it. This begins with sequencing. Sequencing involves breaking strands of DNA into chunks to decode the exact order of the bases in DNA chains. Knowing the order of the bases is the first step to understanding what the various genes that make up the genome do, how different genes are related, and how the various parts of the genome work together.

In 1990, scientists began a massive project called the Human Genome Project. For 13 years, thousands of scientists around the world worked together to identify and map all of the human genome's 3 billion base pairs. The result of the Human Genome Project is that scientists have gained a better understanding of the role that genes play in the human body. The project identified the locations of about 20,500 human genes, giving scientists a detailed map of human genes and important information about the structure, organization, and function of genes. Scientists hope that a better understanding of the roles and numbers of genes will help them discover the causes of and cures for specific diseases.

Specific genes occupy points along a chromosome called loci.

THE HUMAN GENOME PROJECT, 3D ANIMATION

Every cell in our bodies contains chromosomes and DNA. This 3D computer-animated video takes you inside DNA to see how we are made. Studying DNA helps scientists better understand life, disease, and heredity.

At the end of each chromosome, a telomere protects the DNA tip. A telomere is a stretch of DNA that acts like the plastic tip on a shoelace. It prevents the chromosome from fraying or from sticking to itself or another chromosome. Like the rest of the chromosome, a telomere is a sequence of DNA made of the four nucleotide bases.

Scientists have noticed that every time a cell divides, its telomere gets shorter. If a telomere gets short enough, the cell can no longer divide. It becomes inactive and "dies." Scientists have found that telomere shortening is linked to aging, cancer, and a higher risk of death. Current research uses mice to understand more about this connection and how to possibly slow the aging process.

ALL ABOUT TRAITS

In genetics, there's a lot of talk about traits. But what exactly is a trait? A trait is a notable feature or quality in a person. Physical traits are physical characteristics such as hair color, skin color, and height. Behavioral traits are characteristics of the way you act. Some traits can cause a person to have an increased risk of getting a certain disease such as sickle cell anemia, cancer, or heart disease. Each of us has a different combination of traits that have been passed down from generation to generation.

Our genes carry instructions for traits. Sometimes, the environment can affect traits. For example, genes determine hair color. But if you spend a lot of time in the sun or get your hair dyed at a beauty salon, your hair color will change. Training can change behavioral traits. An increased risk of disease can be improved by healthy habits. For example, a predisposition to heart disease can be lessened with healthy eating and exercise.

Some traits are controlled by a single pair of genes. A widow's peak is a good example. You have either a widow's peak or a straight hairline at the top of your forehead. There are two alleles for the gene that controls the hairline, W for a dominant widow's peak and w for a recessive straight hairline. A person who has (ww) alleles will have a straight hairline. A person with (WW) alleles will have a widow's peak. But what about a person who inherited one of each allele (Ww)? When this happens, one allele is usually dominant over a recessive allele. The dominant allele masks the recessive allele. In this example, a widow's peak (W) is dominant and masks the straight hairline allele (w). Therefore, a person with (Ww) alleles will have a widow's peak. Unfortunately, most traits are controlled by several genes and are not this simple to understand.

HOW BIG IS YOUR GENOME?

All living things, from bacteria to plants to humans, have genomes. Genome size is measured in picograms (pg), which is equal to one trillionth of a gram. The size of a genome is called the C-value. Organisms with a larger genome have a higher C-value. In this project, you will research and compare the sizes of different genomes.

- **Go online to the Animal Genome Size Database at www.genomesize.com to look up the C-values of different species.** This database lists organisms by species, so you will have to look up the species' name for the organisms you wish to research.

- **Choose 10 organisms to research.** What animals interest you? Find each on the genome database and record their C-values.

- **Once you have the values for all 10 organisms, think of ways you can organize your data.** Can you create a chart that shows each genome size relative to the others?

To investigate more, create a graph that maps out animals and their genome sizes. Which organisms have the biggest genomes? Which have the smallest? Do you notice any patterns? Can you use your data to predict genome size? Go back to the genome database and research other animals to see if you can.

Ideas for Supplies ▼

- Internet access
- pencil and paper

LET'S SEE...WHAT ANIMALS SHOULD I RESEARCH?

WOW!

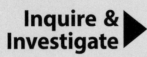

Inquire & Investigate

CREATE A KARYOTYPE

A karyotype is a test that shows a picture of a person's chromosomes. A karyotype reveals if there are any chromosome abnormalities such as extra, missing, or broken chromosomes. Health professionals can use a karyotype to diagnose illness or to determine if a person has a chromosomal abnormality that could be passed on to future children.

To create a karyotype, a geneticist collects cells. When the cells are about to undergo cell division, the chromosomes thicken so that they can be seen clearly under a microscope and photographed. The geneticist then cuts out the chromosomes in the photograph and arranges them in pairs, using size, banding pattern, and centromere position to match pairs. The chromosomes are arranged and numbered by size, from largest to smallest. Then the geneticist examines each pair, looking for chromosome abnormalities.

In this project, you will become a geneticist, creating a karyotype and examining it to see if there are any abnormalities.

- **Photocopy pages 54 and 55.** Cut out the unnumbered chromosomes.

- **Examine each for size, banding, and centromere position.** Find its match among the numbered chromosomes. Repeat until you have matched all of the chromosomes.

- **Study the complete karyotype.** Is the organism male or female? How can you tell? Do you notice any chromosomal abnormalities? If so, what did you find?

KARYOTYPE

Karyotypes are often used to diagnose chromosome abnormalities. What is a karyotype? Watch this short clip to find out!

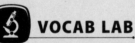 **VOCAB LAB**

Write down what you think each word means: **histones, nucleosome, chromatin, telomere, centromere,** and **karyotype.** Discuss your definitions with friends. Did you all come up with the same definitions? Turn to the text and the glossary if you need help.

DID YOU KNOW?

Humans are incredibly complex organisms, but they do not have the largest genome. Humans have only a few more genes than a chimpanzee or even a mouse. Grasshoppers have about 180 billion base pairs and salamanders have a whopping 765 billion base pairs!

To investigate more, create a karyotype of a patient with a genetic disorder. Have a partner do the same, but do not tell each other what the disorder is. Trade karyotypes and see if you can diagnose the patient. Can you find a chromosome abnormality? What are some of the genetic disorders caused by chromosome abnormalities?

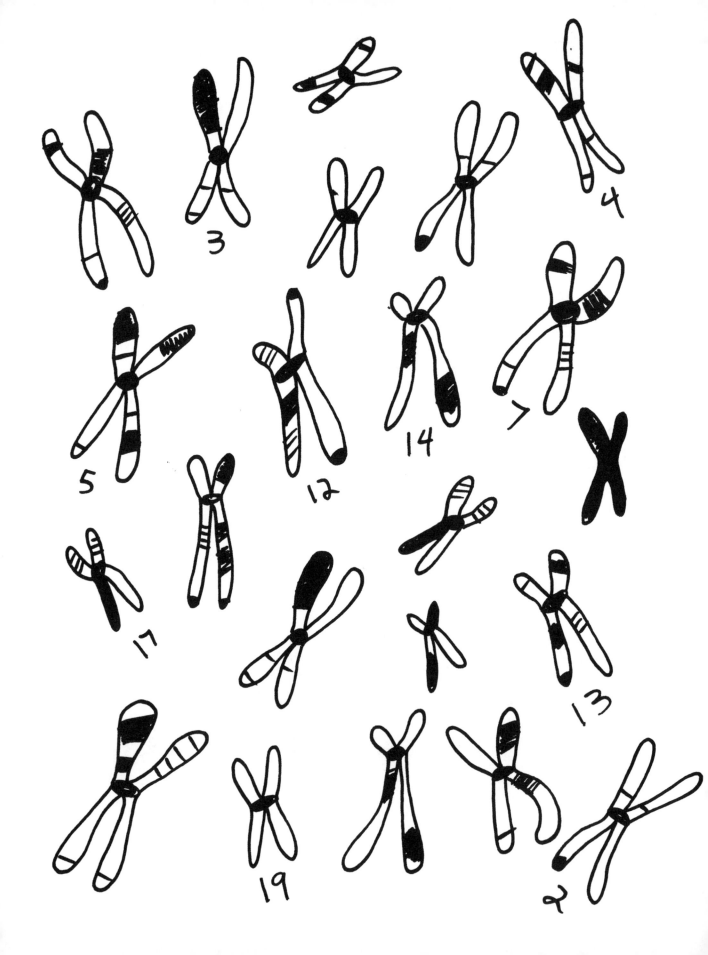

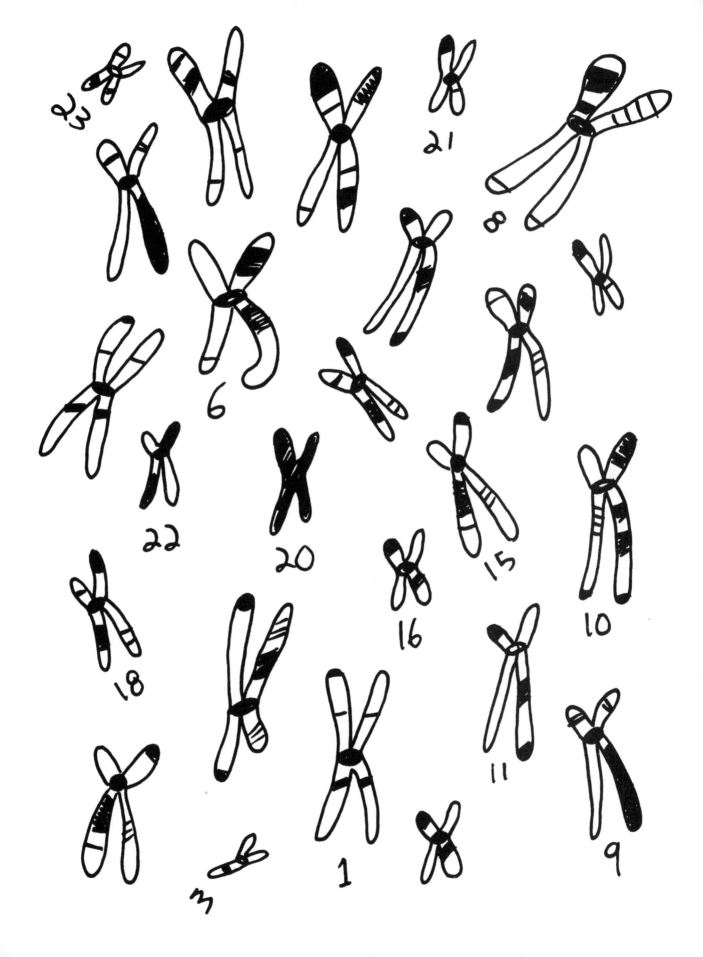

Chapter 5 ▶
Sex Cells and Meiosis

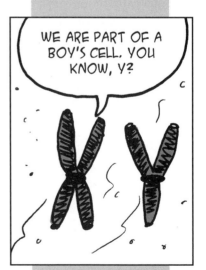

WE ARE PART OF A BOY'S CELL, YOU KNOW, Y?

How are traits passed from parent to child through the chromosomes?

When you were conceived, your mother and father each passed down some of their genes to you. Half came from your mother's egg cell and half came from your father's sperm cell. A baby's gender is controlled by its sex chromosomes. Girls have two X chromosomes, while boys have an X and a Y chromosome.

For some of us, the resemblance to one of our parents is strong. For others, it's not so clear. But if you look closely, you'll probably find that you have some characteristics from your mother and some from your father. They may or may not be obvious, but they're there. For years, people wondered how traits were passed from parent to child. Mendel's experiments proved that factors, which we now know are genes, are passed from parent to offspring and control traits. This passing down of traits is the main idea behind heredity.

A MIX OF GENES

Your mother's egg cell and your father's sperm cell combined to form a cell that developed into a whole new person—you! This cell got half of its genes from your mother and half from your father. Together, these sex cells formed a zygote with a full set of 23 homologous pairs of chromosomes. The zygote then divided multiple times and developed into a baby.

The genes that parents pass to their offspring are random, so each offspring has a unique set of chromosomes. That's why there is no one else like you in the world, unless you have an identical twin. No matter how many offspring the same parents have, their chromosomes will always combine in a different way to produce a unique child. Because every offspring has his or her own mix of chromosomes, the traits they exhibit are also unique. Some traits may take after the father, while others take after the mother, and still others combine into something completely new. That's how you got your mom's nose and your dad's ears, but no one in the family has seen hair like yours!

Most human cells are known as somatic cells. When a somatic cell divides through mitosis, it creates two diploid daughter cells, each with 46 chromosomes. Reproductive cells, however, are different. They are haploid, containing only half of a complete set of chromosomes. To divide, reproductive cells undergo a special type of cell division called meiosis.

MEIOSIS

In sexually reproducing organisms, meiosis starts in diploid cells with a full set of the organism's chromosomes. The cell prepares for meiosis the same way it does for mitosis—by making a copy of its chromosomes. But unlike in mitosis, where the cell divides once, during meiosis there are two cell divisions. The chromosomes duplicate once, then the cell divides twice to produce four gametes, each with one copy of each chromosome. A gamete is a reproductive cell, such as a sperm cell or an egg cell. These haploid gametes do not divide further, but instead join with a gamete from a partner to form a zygote.

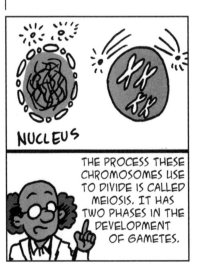

NUCLEUS

THE PROCESS THESE CHROMOSOMES USE TO DIVIDE IS CALLED MEIOSIS. IT HAS TWO PHASES IN THE DEVELOPMENT OF GAMETES.

IN PHASE ONE, MEIOSIS I, HOMOLOGOUS CHROMOSOMES PAIR UP AND FORM TWO HAPLOID CELLS. DNA IS CROSSED DURING THIS PHASE.

Pat Pat

IN MEIOSIS II, THE CHROMOSOMES SPLIT AGAIN, INTO FOUR HAPLOID GAMETE CELLS, THESE ARE THEN READY TO MAKE A NEW LIFE.

The process of meiosis occurs in two stages, meiosis I and meiosis II. In meiosis I, the chromosomes have already replicated. Now they thicken and shorten, becoming visible under the microscope. The duplicated homologous chromosomes pair together as a tetrad. At this point, some crossing-over occurs between the paired-up chromosomes and there is an exchange of genes. This creates chromosomes that are mixed up and are not identical copies of the originals, as happens in diploid cell mitosis.

Meiotic spindles attach to the chromatid pairs and pull them into alignment at the center of the cell. The spindles then pull one homologous chromosome to one pole while other spindles pull the other homologous chromosome to the other pole. Then the cell divides into two new haploid cells, each with a pair of sister chromatids. After a very brief interphase, the two cells prepare for a second division.

In meiosis II, the DNA in the two cells condenses and forms short chromosomes. The sister chromatids line up along the center of the cell, then they split apart into single chromosomes and move to the opposite poles. Nuclear membranes form around the single chromosomes at each end and cell division takes place. At the end of the process, there are now four haploid gamete cells, each containing a single set of 23 chromosomes. Each now has half the DNA needed to make a functioning cell. In reproduction, the gamete from one parent will join with another haploid gamete cell from the other parent. Once joined together, the resulting zygote will have a complete set of DNA on 46 chromosomes.

CROSSING OVER

Another way that organisms encourage genetic variations is through crossing over between homologous chromosomes. Crossing over is a physical exchange of the same segments on chromosomes from mom and dad. During meiosis I, homologous chromosomes pair up and become attached to one another. At this time, sections of DNA move between connected homologous chromosomes.

Crossing over allows for the recombination of DNA on homologous chromosomes. It allows genes to be sorted and inherited independently from one another even though they started on the same chromosome. This is why you might have inherited your hair color from your father even though your eye color comes from your mother.

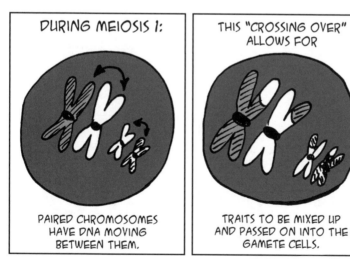

DURING MEIOSIS 1:

PAIRED CHROMOSOMES HAVE DNA MOVING BETWEEN THEM.

THIS "CROSSING OVER" ALLOWS FOR

TRAITS TO BE MIXED UP AND PASSED ON INTO THE GAMETE CELLS.

GENETIC VARIATION

Meiosis encourages genetic variety in offspring. One way it generates organisms with genetic variety is by allowing the many different ways the maternal and paternal chromosomes can combine in the haploid gametes. In humans, with 23 chromosome pairs, there are more than 8 million possible combinations of chromosomes.

 Wondering about meiosis? You can watch this clip to learn more about this special type of cell division that is necessary for sexual reproduction in eukaryotic organisms.

MEIOSIS CAN GO WRONG

Most of the time, the process of meiosis goes according to plan. In a small number of cases, however, something goes wrong. Sometimes chromosomes are not divided equally into gametes. When this happens, one gamete may get two copies of a chromosome, while another gamete gets nothing.

BOY OR GIRL?

In humans, the trait that determines if you are male or female is controlled by two sex chromosomes: X and Y. Females have two X chromosomes (XX), while males have an X and a Y chromosome (XY). When haploid gametes are created in meiosis, each has one sex chromosome, either an X or a Y. When two gametes join in reproduction, the combination of sex chromosomes determines the offspring's gender.

If the sex chromosomes are XX, the offspring will be a female. If they are XY, the offspring will be a male. Because females only have two X chromosomes, gametes from the mother always carry an X chromosome. However, males (XY) can pass either an X or a Y chromosome to their offspring. Therefore, it's the father's gamete that actually determines whether the offspring is a boy or a girl!

EACH PARENT HAS A PAIR OF SEX CHROMOSOMES THAT MAKE UP HIS OR HER PHYSICAL GENDER.

ONLY MEN HAVE THE "Y" CHROMOSOME, SO IF A "Y" FERTILIZES THE EGG...

...ANOTHER MALE WILL BE BORN INTO THE WORLD. ONLY THE DAD'S "X" OR "Y" CAN DETERMINE THE CHILD'S GENDER.

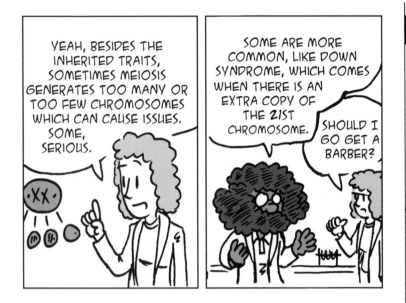

SEX-LINKED TRAITS

In addition to determining whether an offspring is male or female, sex chromosomes carry several other genes. Traits that are controlled by genes located on the sex chromosomes are called sex-linked traits. Genes on the X chromosome control X-linked traits. In humans, some recessive disorders such as colorblindness are linked to the X chromosome. These disorders rarely affect women, because if a woman has the recessive gene for colorblindness on one of her X chromosomes, she probably has a gene for normal vision on her other X chromosome that will mask the recessive trait. Her male offspring, however, may not be so lucky. If the woman has one copy of the recessive gene, she is a carrier. She has a 50/50 chance of passing the X chromosome with the recessive gene to her son. If her son inherits the recessive X, he will be colorblind, because he does not have another X chromosome with a gene to mask the recessive gene and the Y chromosome does not carry the trait for color vision.

WHAT HAPPENS WHEN MEIOSIS GOES WRONG?

If a person has the wrong number of chromosomes, the missing or extra genetic information often causes a genetic disorder. If a gamete with an extra chromosome joins another gamete with normal chromosome numbers in fertilization, the resulting zygote will have three copies of one chromosome, resulting in 47 total chromosomes. This condition is called a trisomy. Down syndrome is the most common chromosomal disorder and is caused by a trisomy of chromosome 21. If a gamete with a missing chromosome joins a normal gamete, the resulting zygote will have only one copy of a chromosome, resulting in 45 total chromosomes. This is a monosomy.

MITOSIS

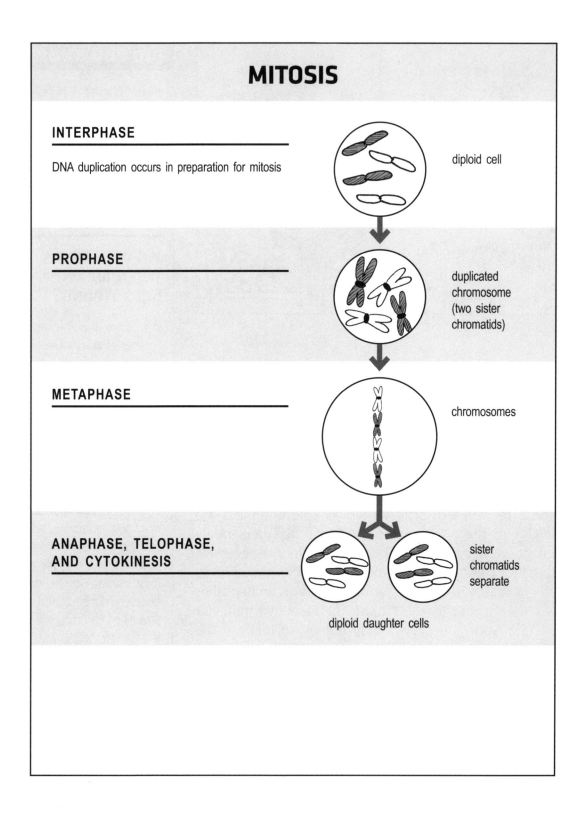

INTERPHASE

DNA duplication occurs in preparation for mitosis

diploid cell

PROPHASE

duplicated
chromosome
(two sister
chromatids)

METAPHASE

chromosomes

**ANAPHASE, TELOPHASE,
AND CYTOKINESIS**

sister
chromatids
separate

diploid daughter cells

MEIOSIS

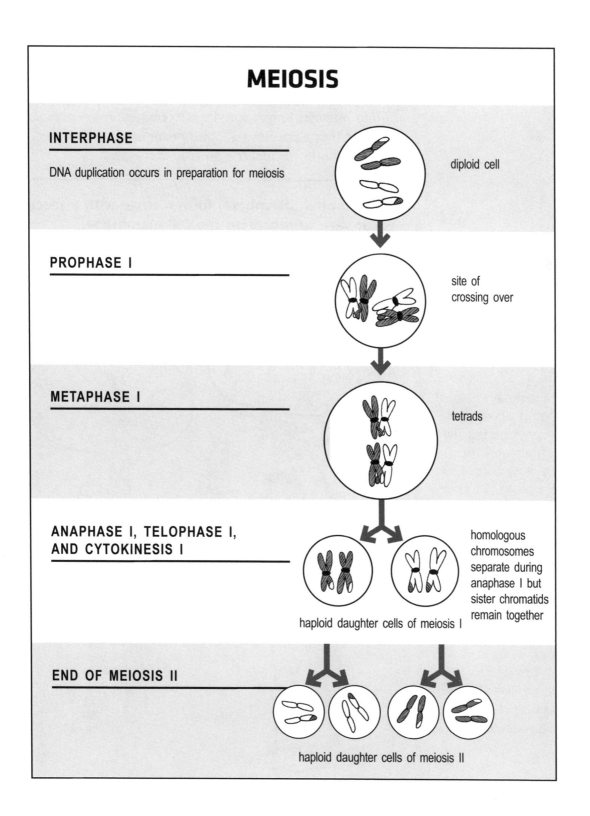

INTERPHASE

DNA duplication occurs in preparation for meiosis

diploid cell

PROPHASE I

site of
crossing over

METAPHASE I

tetrads

**ANAPHASE I, TELOPHASE I,
AND CYTOKINESIS I**

homologous
chromosomes
separate during
anaphase I but
sister chromatids
remain together

haploid daughter cells of meiosis I

END OF MEIOSIS II

haploid daughter cells of meiosis II

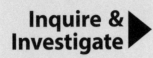
CREATE A MEIOSIS MODEL

Cells produce gametes through the process of meiosis. During meiosis, one parent cell creates four haploid gametes that each have 23 chromosomes. In this project, you will visually model the process of meiosis.

- **To model interphase, form a circle with a piece of yarn to represent the cell membrane.**

- **Cut pipe cleaners and make four chromosomes, each in a different color.** Place each into the cell, representing the cell in its normal state.

FROM GAMETE TO ZYGOTE

Reproductive cells have only half of a complete set of chromosomes. They undergo a special cell division process called meiosis for this to happen. A gamete is a reproductive cell, either an egg cell from the mother or a sperm cell from the father. Each gamete is haploid, holding half of the organism's DNA. In reproduction, the gamete from one parent joins the gamete from the other parent. The resulting zygote will have a complete set of DNA.

- **Right before the cell divides, what happens to the chromosomes?** Add matching doubles of your chromosomes to the cell and twist each pair of doubles together so that they are joined as a unit.

- **Line up pairs of homologous chromosomes together along the center of the cell.** Then separate the pairs so that one of each pair moves to the opposite side of the cell.

- **Adjust the yarn to show the cell dividing into separate cells.** How many cells have formed? How many chromosomes are in each cell? What do they look like?

- **As the cells enter meiosis II, line up the chromosomes in your cell as you would expect them to prepare for this phase.** Are they along the middle line, at the poles, or floating around? Do they double?

- **Separate the two pieces of each chromosome pair.** Move each piece toward opposite poles in the cell.

- **As each cell divides again, move the yarn to circle the new cells.** How many cells are there now? How many chromosomes does each have?

To investigate more, compare the chromosomes of each of the gametes. Are they the same or different? How do they compare to the chromosomes in the original parent cell?

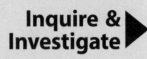
MODEL CROSSING OVER

Mendel proposed the Law of Independent Assortment, stating that genes are inherited independently of one another. Yet there are many genes located on a chromosome. If two genes are on the same chromosome, then they might be inherited as a unit during meiosis. The process of crossing over that occurs during meiosis allows genes to sort independently.

At the beginning of meiosis, a replicated chromosome finds its homologous match, the same chromosome inherited from the other parent. The two homologous chromosomes stick together as a tetrad. At this point, genes on one arm of one chromosome can cross over or switch places with genes on the arm of the homologous chromosome. When this happens, a gene from your father's original chromosome may cross over to the arm of your mother's chromosome. Her matching gene moves from her chromosome to the father's chromosome, and perfectly replaces the missing gene. As a result, when the homologous pairs separate, the father's gene is now on the chromosome from the mother. This ensures that genes do not have to be inherited as a unit, but can sort independently of other genes. In this project, you will model the process of crossing over during meiosis.

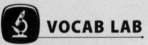 Crossing over is a physical exchange of the same segments on chromosomes from mom and dad. It occurs during meiosis I.

🔬 VOCAB LAB

Write down what you think each word means: **somatic, diploid, haploid, meiosis, gamete, zygote, tetrad, autosomal,** and **crossing over.** Discuss your definitions with friends. Did you all come up with the same definitions? Turn to the text and the glossary if you need help.

- **Use clay to create two chromosomes.** How can you use different colors to represent chromosomes inherited from the mother and chromosomes inherited from the father?

- **Use more colored pieces of clay.** Make two separate genes on the mother's chromosome and two separate genes on the father's chromosome.

- **Before meiosis begins, the chromosomes replicate.** Can you create two exact copies of your chromosomes? Where do the copies attach to the original chromosomes?

- **Line up the homologous chromosomes and attach to form a tetrad so that crossing over can occur.** Gently remove one of the genes from the mother's chromosome and switch it with a gene on the father's chromosome.

- **Modeling the phases of meiosis, separate the homologous pairs.** Then separate the attached sister chromatids and create gamete cells.

- **What does the DNA and chromosome look like in each of your four gamete cells?** How is it different than the chromosome and genes prior to crossing over?

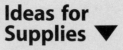

To investigate more, repeat the crossing over model and vary the genes that will move. How do the resulting chromosomes differ from the ones formed in your first model? How does crossing over affect the diversity of offspring?

CREATE A FAMILY PEDIGREE

A pedigree is a chart that can show phenotypes of individuals in a family to highlight how a trait is inherited. Pedigrees can track the way a trait is passed down through generations. They can be used for horses, dogs, or even humans.

Pedigree charts are made using shapes and lines. Males are drawn as squares, while females are draw as circles. If an individual expresses a trait, his or her square or circle is colored. If the individual is a carrier, the square or circle is half-colored. The lines show relationships between individuals. Vertical lines separate generations. A horizontal line connects a male and female that are parents together. Siblings are shown by shapes attached to vertical lines that are connected by a horizontal line.

In this experiment, you will select a trait and trace it through your family. With the information you learn, you will draw a pedigree.

🧬 **When studying a pedigree, it is helpful to remember certain patterns in heredity. If a trait appears equally in males and females, it is probably located on an autosomal chromosome. A trait that appears in every generation is probably dominant. A trait that skips generations is probably recessive. Traits that appear more frequently in males are usually sex-linked.**

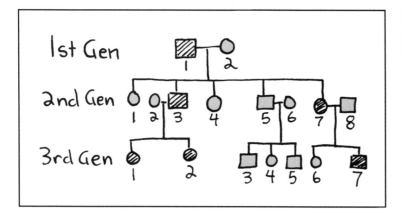

- **Decide what trait you want to investigate in your family.** What are some of the common traits you've noticed? Some ideas include eye color, attached earlobes, ability to roll the tongue, widow's peak, dimples, cleft chin, and color blindness. You may also choose an unusual trait that is present in your family.

- **Using the symbols in the chart, draw a pedigree of your family.** How many people and generations can you include?

- **Gather information about each individual.** Does he or she have the trait you are studying? For each person who has the trait, color in his or her shape on the pedigree.

- **After you have finished, study the pedigree.** How often was the trait expressed? Do you think it is autosomal dominant, autosomal recessive, or a sex-linked trait? Why?

To investigate more, select one couple in your pedigree. If they were to have another child, what is your prediction for the probability that the child would express the trait? How did you come to this prediction?

Ideas for Supplies ▼

- several generations of family members to interview
- paper
- pencil

Traits controlled by genes on the sex chromosomes are called sex-linked traits. Some recessive disorders such as colorblindness and hemophilia are sex-linked traits controlled by the X chromosome.

INHERITANCE OF TRAITS

Parents pass traits to their offspring through genes, a process that is the basis of heredity. In this experiment, you will examine four traits with a partner and produce two "offspring." Using your knowledge of meiosis and the laws of inheritance, you will predict the genotypes and phenotypes of your future "children."

- **Create a chart for four traits you will examine. Examples include widow's peak, tongue roller, and dimples.** You will need columns for your phenotype and genotype and your partner's phenotype and genotype. For the purpose of this activity, if you have a dominant trait, make the genotype heterozygous.

- **Write your genotype alleles on the square pieces of paper, using a different color paper for each trait.** The squares will represent chromosomes. Write each allele on a different square of paper. For example, if your genotype for the dimples trait is Dd, then you would write D on one paper and d on a second paper of the same color. Because chromosomes double before meiosis begins, you will need to create a second set of papers to represent your doubled chromosome. Your partner should do the same for his or her traits, using the same colored paper squares.

- **Line up your homologous pairs and separate them randomly into two piles.** Each pile should have two sister chromatids for each color of squares. This completes meiosis I.

- **Next, separate the sister chromatids into individual squares.** You need to end up with four piles, each of which represents possible gametes.

- **Choose one of your gametes and have your partner choose a gamete from his or her piles.** Congratulations! You're now the proud parents of a new baby!

- **Create a chart for your baby that includes columns for the allele from you and the allele from your partner for each trait.** What genotype is the baby for each trait? What phenotype?

- **Repeat the process for a second child.** How are the traits similar or different between the two offspring?

Ideas for Supplies ▼

- partner
- paper
- pencil
- small squares of colored construction paper
- stapler

To investigate more, join with another pair of partners and become "grandparents" by combining one of your offspring with one of theirs to create a "grandchild." What phenotypes and genotypes does the grandchild have? Which grandparent do you think the child most resembles? Why?

USE A PUNNETT SQUARE TO PREDICT TRAITS IN OFFSPRING

A Punnett square is a tool you can use to predict the offspring of genetic crosses. Animal breeders, farmers, geneticists, and others use Punnett squares to predict how likely it is that an offspring will inherit a specific set of alleles. The square is divided into four parts. One parent's alleles are written across the top of the square. The other parent's alleles are written down the side of the square. All possible combinations of genes are shown in the four sections of the square. In this experiment, you will use a Punnett square to predict the offspring of a cross between two dogs. Then you will simulate the actual cross and compare your results.

- **Draw a Punnett square for the cross between two black dogs.** Assume that each dog is heterozygous for the black coat trait (B), but also carries a recessive allele for a white coat (b). Draw a box and divide it into four sections. Write the alleles for one parent across the top, and the alleles for the other parent down the side. Fill in the possible allele combinations in the four sections.

HMM...IF YOU HAVE PUPPIES WITH ANOTHER BLACK DOG, I WONDER WHAT YOUR PUPPIES WOULD LOOK LIKE. SOUNDS LIKE I COULD DO AN EXPERIMENT TO FIND OUT...

HOW TO DRAW A PUNNETT SQUARE

You've read about Punnett squares. Now you can watch this video to learn how to create your own!

- **Based on your Punnett square, what percentage of offspring do you expect to be heterozygous dominant (Bb)?** What about homozygous dominant (BB) and homozygous recessive (bb)? If these dogs had a litter of eight puppies how many would you expect to have each genotype? What phenotypes would the puppies have?

- **To simulate the actual cross, label one of the cups "Dad" and the other "Mom."** Place one black bead and one white bead in each cup. Without looking, pull one bead from each cup. These beads represent the alleles for the first puppy. Record the puppy's genotype. Replace the beads in their respective cups and repeat for the litter's remaining seven puppies.

- **What percentage of the litter had each genotype —BB, Bb, and bb?** What percentage of the litter had a black coat phenotype and what percent had a white coat phenotype? How do these results compare to your Punnett square predictions? How do you explain your results? What do you predict would happen if you "created" 50 more puppies? Why?

To investigate more, design a Punnett square to predict the outcomes for a two-trait cross. Then simulate the actual cross with beads or other household objects. How do your results compare to your prediction? Why?

Ideas for Supplies ▼

- 2 pennies
- paper
- pencil

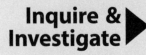 Tossed individually, each penny has an equal chance of landing on heads or tails. Each outcome has a 50 percent probability of occurring. When you toss both pennies at the same time, what is the probability of two heads landing at the same time? Two tails? What is the probability of one head and one tail?

PROBABILITY AND HEREDITY

What role does probability play in heredity? Humans have two of each chromosome. When gametes join for reproduction, chance determines which chromosomes will be combined in the offspring. Each chromosome has a 50 percent chance of being passed to the offspring. If you know the alleles of the parents, you can use the laws of probability to predict how likely it is that offspring will inherit specific alleles.

- **Each penny represents gametes from a parent who is heterozygous dominant for the tallness trait.** Heads represents the dominant allele (T), while tails represents the recessive allele (t).

- **Before you begin tossing the coins, make some predictions.** After 12 tosses, what results do you predict? After 50 tosses, what results do you predict? What about after 100 tosses?

- **Now, toss the coins together and record the results in a data table.** How do your actual results compare to your predictions after 12, 50, and 100 tosses? How do you explain your results? How does the number of tosses affect the actual results compared to the predicted results?

> To investigate more, add a nickel to represent a second, independent trait. What do you predict will happen when you toss the two coins together? Toss the coins and record your results. How do your actual results compare to your prediction?

Chapter 6
Sending Messages

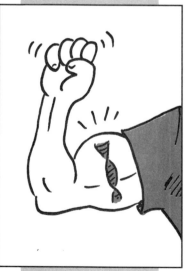

How does DNA
work to keep our
bodies healthy and
functioning well?

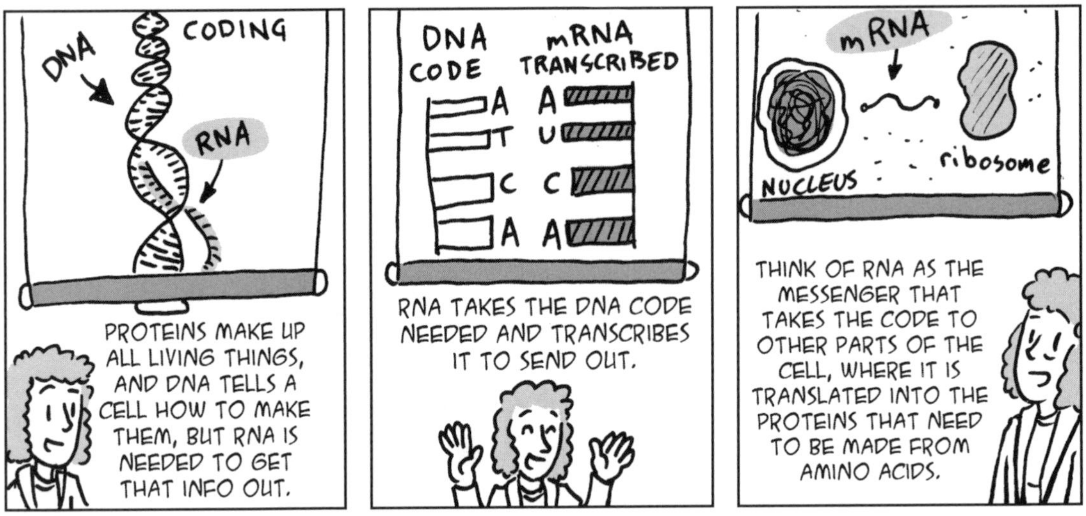
DNA
CODING
RNA
PROTEINS MAKE UP ALL LIVING THINGS, AND DNA TELLS A CELL HOW TO MAKE THEM, BUT RNA IS NEEDED TO GET THAT INFO OUT.
DNA CODE
mRNA TRANSCRIBED
A A
T U
C C
A A
RNA TAKES THE DNA CODE NEEDED AND TRANSCRIBES IT TO SEND OUT.
mRNA
NUCLEUS
ribosome
THINK OF RNA AS THE MESSENGER THAT TAKES THE CODE TO OTHER PARTS OF THE CELL, WHERE IT IS TRANSLATED INTO THE PROTEINS THAT NEED TO BE MADE FROM AMINO ACIDS.

We need proteins to run our cells and our bodies. DNA uses information in the genes to make all of the proteins we need. Each gene contains instructions to make a protein.

DNA holds the instructions that control an organism's traits. They tell the cell how to build the proteins that control not only how we look or how we act, but also healthy functioning of our organs. Proteins are the building blocks of all living things and making proteins is one of DNA's main functions.

What is a protein? You're probably aware of the importance of eating protein through foods like meat, fish, eggs, dairy, nuts, and beans. Here's why. Our body breaks down proteins to build and maintain all the cells and tissues in our body. Most muscles and organs are made up mostly of protein. In fact, proteins are responsible for almost all of the body's processes. If you don't eat enough protein, your body won't be able to fix old cells that are damaged or build new ones.

In the human body, there are about 100 trillion cells, each of which is responsible for a specific job. Within each cell, there are thousands of proteins working together to run the cell. Special proteins called actin and myosin allow your muscle cells to contract. Enzymes in your stomach are proteins that digest food. Growth hormones are proteins that tell your bones to grow. Proteins also carry out bodily functions such as digestion and respiration.

BUILDING BLUEPRINT

Cells use the information coded in their genes as a blueprint for making proteins. Each gene contains instructions to make a protein. A cell's protein building takes place in the cytoplasm, outside of the nucleus. So how does the protein factory get the blueprint when DNA is hidden inside the cell nucleus? DNA sends a message!

When a cell needs to make a protein, special equipment in the cell's nucleus reads the gene and sends a message using messenger RNA (mRNA), a molecule that is very similar to DNA. Carrying the message, mRNA moves out of the cell nucleus and into the cytoplasm through holes in the nuclear membrane called nuclear pores. Once it reaches the cytoplasm, the cell's protein-making factories, the ribosomes, read the message and produce the protein. Once made, the protein travels to the part of the cell where it is needed and gets to work.

JUNK DNA

Did you know that less than 2 percent of your total DNA carries instructions to make proteins? The rest of your DNA is composed of non-coding sequences, sometimes called junk DNA. The name "junk" can be misleading, however. Scientists believe that many of these non-coding sequences actually have very important functions. Some non-coding sequences regulate when and where genes are expressed. Some sequences may determine chromosome structure or play a role in meiosis. Other sequences determine how much of a protein is created in a cell or where transcription factors attach to a DNA strand. So although it is called junk DNA, it may actually be quite useful!

DNA STRUCTURE AND REPLICATION

DNA stores our genetic instructions. In humans, every body cell contains DNA. What does it look like? How does it copy itself? You can watch this video to find out more!

WHAT EXACTLY IS RNA?

RNA, or ribonucleic acid, is very similar to DNA. Like DNA, RNA is made from a sugar (ribose), a phosphate, and four nucleotide bases. Three of RNA's bases are the same as DNA's: adenine, guanine, and cytosine. Instead of thymine, however, RNA uses a fourth base called uracil. When RNA is forming, uracil takes thymine's place and bonds with adenine.

Although RNA is like DNA in many ways, there are also a few differences. DNA is very strong and stable, while RNA is unstable and decomposes quickly. RNA is usually a single strand, instead of DNA's double strand.

There are three main types of RNA, all of which have a role in creating proteins: mRNA carries a message from DNA out of the cell nucleus, tRNA carries amino acids to translate the message, and rRNA puts the amino acids together into chains that build a protein.

A CHAIN OF AMINO ACIDS

So how does DNA send its message? First of all, proteins come in many shapes and sizes, but all are a chain of amino acids. Amino acids are organic compounds that contain nitrogen and carbon.

There are 20 amino acids that combine together in thousands of unique combinations to create proteins. The amino acid chains are folded into complex shapes and hooked together. The sequence of the amino acids in the chain determines the structure of the protein. One protein molecule contains as many as 5,000 amino acids.

The DNA sequence of bases is the code that tells the cell the order of amino acids for each protein. Because the four bases alone are not enough to code for 20 different amino acids, the bases combine into groups of three. This creates 64 possible combinations of three-base groups, which is more than enough to code for 20 different amino acids.

A group of three bases is known as a codon, which is like a word in the language of DNA. Because there are 64 possible codons, more than one codon can code for the same amino acid. In addition, some codons are used to signal the end of a chain of amino acids, while the codon A-U-G is usually used to signal the beginning of a chain.

TRANSCRIPTION

Protein-building requires two steps: transcription and translation. In genetics, transcription is the process of recording DNA's message in the language of RNA. Transcription keeps DNA safe in the cell's nucleus but sends an RNA copy into the cell's cytoplasm. In transcription, the DNA code is copied to a strand of mRNA. A single gene may be transcribed thousands of times, every time the protein it codes for is needed.

Before a gene can be transcribed, it must be located. Chromosomes have about 3 billion base pairs and contain from 20,000 to 25,000 genes. Finding the right one sounds like looking for a needle in a haystack!

Fortunately, DNA has an easy way to find the right genes. Before transcription begins, proteins called transcription factors bind to a region of the DNA called the promoter. The promoter identifies where a gene starts, which strand is to be copied, and in which direction it should be copied.

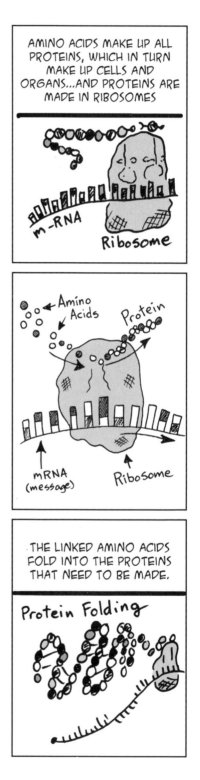

AMINO ACIDS MAKE UP ALL PROTEINS, WHICH IN TURN MAKE UP CELLS AND ORGANS...AND PROTEINS ARE MADE IN RIBOSOMES

m-RNA
Ribosome

Amino Acids
Protein
mRNA (message)
Ribosome

THE LINKED AMINO ACIDS FOLD INTO THE PROTEINS THAT NEED TO BE MADE.

Protein Folding

BUILDING PROTEINS

Messenger RNA (mRNA) carries DNA's message out of the cell's nucleus to the ribosomes, which read the message and produce proteins. Transcription is the process by which DNA's information is transferred to mRNA. During transcription, mRNA creates a single-strand copy of DNA. After mRNA is formed, it moves out of the cell's nucleus into cytoplasm, where it will be translated into a protein.

The enzyme RNA polymerase binds to the transcription factors and the promoter and unwinds the DNA. Then the RNA polymerase organizes nucleotides that complement the bases in the DNA strand being copied. Transcription ends when RNA polymerase finds the terminator, which acts as a stop sign to signal the end of a gene. Thus, a strand of mRNA has been formed.

Before mRNA heads out of the cell nucleus carrying DNA's message, it gets a cap and tail. The cap and tail help mRNA move through the nuclear pore, protect it during its journey, and help ribosomes attach during translation.

TRANSLATION

The second step of protein building is called translation, which takes place in the cell's cytoplasm. Translation is the process of decoding the mRNA message created during transcription into working proteins. Each three-base code, such as U-G-C, in the RNA message is a codon representing a single amino acid.

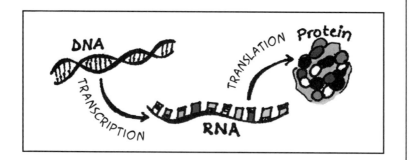

The entire strand of mRNA carries the words for many amino acids. The mRNA sequence is used as a template to assemble—in order—the chain of amino acids that link together to form a single protein.

When mRNA reaches the cytoplasm, a ribosome recognizes it and latches onto its cap. The ribosome scans the mRNA to find the start codon, located in the promoter region, where translation should begin. The transfer RNA, or tRNA, floating around in the cytoplasm contains the anticodons that match up with the codons on the mRNA. When the anticodon interacts with the complementary codon of the mRNA, the ribosome adds the resulting attached amino acid to the end of the growing protein.

The ribosome keeps adding amino acids until it reaches the stop codon in the mRNA message. The completed protein is clipped off by a ribosomal enzyme and released. After it is released, the amino acid chain folds to become a mature protein. The ribosome also releases the mRNA strand, and then looks for another mRNA to begin another translation and the creation of another protein.

DNA Translation uses the genetic information carried by mRNA to build proteins. It is the second major step in gene expression, after transcription. During translation, mRNA is read in groups of three-base pairs called a codon. Each codon calls for a specific amino acid. The chain of amino acids builds a protein.

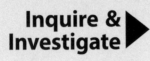

SEND AN RNA MESSAGE

Messenger RNA (mRNA) makes a copy of a piece of DNA in the cell's nucleus. It carries the message from the nucleus into the cell's cytoplasm, where the message's instructions are used to build a protein. In this project, you will create an mRNA message.

- **If you have the DNA strand from the DNA replication activity in Chapter 3, you can use it here and skip down to the fourth step.** If not, you can create a new DNA strand by cutting the construction paper into several strips approximately 1 inch across and 6 inches long. Repeat for each color of paper.

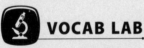

VOCAB LAB

Write down what you think each word means: **proteins, ribonucleic acid (RNA), amino acid, codon, transcription, translation,** and **promoter**. Discuss your definitions with friends. Did you all come up with the same definitions? Turn to the text and the glossary if you need help.

- construction paper in eight different colors
- scissors
- tape or stapler

- **Using the construction paper strips, create rings and link them together to form a DNA ladder.** What does each color represent? Where are the sugars, the phosphate groups, the four bases, and the hydrogen bonds in your DNA ladder?

- **Now that you have created a DNA model, simulate replication.** What is the first step in replication? What does your model look like after you complete this step?

- **Now simulate the mRNA copying a segment of the DNA chain.** Sever the hydrogen bond between the bases on several ladder rungs.

- **Recreate the missing side and rungs using complementary bases.** Which base is replaced with uracil? Use a different colored strip to represent the uracil base in mRNA. You've made an mRNA message!

To investigate more, take your mRNA message to the ribosome. How will the ribosome and tRNA work to translate the message into a protein? Write down the sequence of bases that your message carries. Separate these bases into three-base codons. Research what amino acid corresponds to each codon. What is the sequence of amino acids in the protein you created?

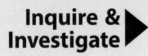

BUILD A PROTEIN

**Ideas for
Supplies ▼**

- pencil
- paper
- copy of the
  Universal
  Genetic Code
  from the Internet

Cells use the processes of transcription and translation to read the instructions in a gene and link a chain of amino acids that becomes a protein. Each protein is created by a specific combination of 20 different amino acids. Using the Universal Genetic Code, you will translate a gene into a protein.

- **When transcription starts, a portion of the DNA ladder unzips so that mRNA can copy the gene's sequence of nucleotide bases.** Here is the sequence of unzipped DNA that you will use:

  A T T A C C A C C T G G T C A C G A T T C T

- **How can you transcribe this code?** What is the complementary base that mRNA will use to create the gene's message?

- **The ribosomes, which are the cell's protein-making factories, take mRNA's message and translate it to build an amino acid chain.** The ribosome begins at the start codon A-U-G, and then reads the nucleotides in three-base codons. Can you find the start codon in your message? Can you translate your message by finding the correct amino acid for each RNA codon in the chain?

- **When the ribosome reaches a stop codon (U-A-A, U-A-G, U-G-A) in the mRNA message, it knows that it has finished building the amino acid chain.** When you find a stop codon in your message, you have finished building the protein!

ALL THESE CODES, I FEEL LIKE A SPY!

DNA CODE

To investigate more, repeat transcribing the DNA strand, but this time make an error in the transcription. How does this error affect the amino acid chain and resulting protein? Are there some errors that would not affect the amino acid chain? Why?

Chapter 7 ▶
Gene Mutations

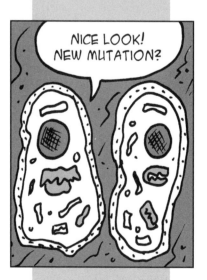

How do
mutations occur?

DNA A mutation occurs when there is a change in a gene's DNA sequence of nucleotides. Gene mutations are rare, occurring in about one of every 100,000 genes. Since humans have about 200,000 genes, that means you probably are carrying an average of two mutations in your genes!

We know that an error that occurs during cell division can cause a person to have too many or too few chromosomes. Sometimes a chromosome has an error within it. Most of the time, genes stay the same as they pass from cell to cell or parent to child. Occasionally, though, genes mutate and there is a permanent change in a gene because of a change in its DNA sequence of nucleotides.

A change in one nucleotide in a long string of DNA may not seem like a big deal. Yet a mutation in just one nucleotide can have a real effect on an organism. When building proteins, the DNA sequence is read in groups of three nucleotides. Each group of three nucleotide bases, called a codon, codes for a specific amino acid. You can think of the DNA sequence as a series of three-letter words. Each word calls for a specific amino acid in a protein.

This example shows how a minor change in the sequence can be so dramatic:

Themanwasoldbuttheboywasnot.

If you read this sentence correctly using three-letter groups, it says:

> The man was old but the boy was not.

If this sentence was a gene, each letter would be a nucleotide base and each word would be a codon. But what would happen if one of the letters from this sentence was missing? If you deleted the "h" from "the," the sentence might read like this:

> Tem anw aso ldb utt heb oyw asn ot.

What if you added an extra letter, such as an "x" to "man"?

> The mxa nwa sol dbu tth ebo ywa sno t.

In both cases, the sentence becomes unreadable. In the same way, one small mutation or change in the nucleotide sequence can make a gene unreadable.

WHAT TYPES OF MUTATIONS OCCUR?

Sometimes a mutation occurs because the wrong base is used in the DNA sequence. This type of substitution error can be passed on to future cells in mitosis. The error in the DNA will be copied incorrectly, over and over again. The wrong base can also change the codon and resulting amino acid used when building a protein. Sometimes, the wrong base still codes for the necessary protein and has no effect on the organism. Other times, a substitution error that creates a stop codon ends the protein chain too soon.

MUTATIONS

Mutations are changes in DNA. To find out more about what mutations are, how they happen, and if they are good or bad, watch this short video.

UM...THIS IS A PHOTO COPIER...

YEAH, WELL...

WHEN A GENE SEQUENCE UNDERGOES MITOSIS THE CODE IS COPIED EXACTLY, BUT SOMETIMES THE CODE CHANGES, OR MUTATES, AND GETS COPIED OVER AND OVER...

GOOD MUTATIONS?

Not all mutations are bad. In rare cases, a mutation in the genetic code causes a protein to work better than it did before the mutation. The organism may be better able to live in its environment than others without the mutation. When this occurs, the mutation is called an adaptation. Through beneficial mutations or adaptations, evolution is possible.

Mutations can also occur when an entire nucleotide base is added or deleted from the DNA sequence. Insertion and deletion mutations often result in sections of DNA that are unreadable and cannot produce a protein. These mutations are examples of frameshift mutations, which change the three-letter reading frame for the DNA sequence, resulting in changes to every amino acid after the mutation.

The severity of a mutation depends on how much it changes the amino acids and resulting proteins and eventually affects cell function.

WHAT CAUSES MUTATIONS?

Mutations generally happen in one of two ways. Some cells make a mistake when copying DNA for cell division. These mistakes happen about once in every 100,000,000 bases. Some of these mistakes are corrected by special DNA repair proteins that check the work during DNA replication. If they find a nucleotide that is paired incorrectly, they remove the wrong base and insert the correct one.

Other times, environmental agents called mutagens can damage DNA, resulting in a mutation. Ultraviolet light, radiation, and some chemicals are mutagens that are known to damage DNA by altering nucleotide bases so they end up looking like other nucleotide bases. When the DNA is copied, the damaged base might pair with an incorrect base, causing a mutation. Sometimes mutagens can damage DNA by breaking the bonds between its oxygen and phosphate groups. The DNA tries to repair itself but, unfortunately, is not always successful. Another type of mutation is translocation, which is when parts of different chromosomes join together.

MUTATION EFFECTS

Most of the time, changes caused by a mutated gene are subtle. Either they make no noticeable change in a gene's expression or the changes do not affect the gene's function. Remember that the same amino acid can be coded by several different codons. If the mutation simply changes the codon to another that codes for the same amino acid, the mutation will have no effect. In addition, some sequences of DNA are not part of any gene and do not have a known function. If a mutation occurs in these areas, it will not have a noticeable effect.

Other times, a gene mutation can cause a serious defect. If the amino acid is changed in a crucial part of a protein, it may make the protein unable to perform its function. If a protein cannot do its job, then the cells that use that protein might not be able to work properly. You can think of a cell as a machine with many parts. If one part breaks, it's possible for the machine to still be able to work if the part wasn't that important. But if the part was critical, the entire machine may shut down. In the same way, a cell may still be able to function, depending on which protein malfunctions. Or it may come to a grinding halt.

GENETIC COUNSELORS

For families dealing with a genetic disorder, genetic counselors are specially trained to provide information, counseling, and support. Together with doctors, counselors help families get the latest information about a disorder and understand how it may affect not only the person with the condition, but the family as a whole. For couples at risk of passing a genetic disorder to future generations, genetic counselors can also help them better analyze the real risks involved.

THESE MUTATIONS, ARE THEY REALLY NOTICABLE?

IT DEPENDS ON WHAT PART OF THE GENE HAS THE MUTATION.

BUT, IF THE MUTATION AFFECTS THE EXPRESSION OF THE GENE, IT CAN BE VERY DETRIMENTAL...

HEREDITY AND MUTATIONS

Sometimes mutations are passed from parent to child. When a germline mutation occurs during meiosis in the formation of a reproductive cell, it is passed to offspring. Other mutations occur randomly throughout an organism's lifetime. These somatic mutations are not passed along to offspring. Instead, they only affect the host organism. Most of the time, cells are able to repair somatic mutations as they occur. When they cannot, certain diseases or medical conditions may occur. Most types of cancer are somatic diseases caused by cell mutation. It is sometimes sped up by environmental factors, like cigarette smoking or long-term exposure to the sun.

Fortunately, most mutations are recessive. Recessive mutations are only expressed when a person inherits two mutated genes. Even if one of the genes is mutated, the second chromosome usually has a normal copy that the cell can use to make the protein.

MUTATIONS AND DISEASE

Some mutations are linked to genetic disorders. A genetic disorder is a disease that is caused by an abnormality or mutation in DNA. Single-gene disorders are caused by a mutation of one gene that causes its protein to be missing or changed. Multifactor disorders are caused by mutations in several genes, along with environmental causes.

Most of these rare inherited diseases are recessive, so they only show up if both genes carry the mutation. Some of the most common recessive diseases are cystic fibrosis, sickle cell anemia, and Tay-Sachs disease. Cystic fibrosis is an autosomal recessive disorder that is caused by mutations in a gene on chromosome 7. People with sickle cell anemia have a mutation on chromosome 11 in a gene responsible for making one part of the protein in hemoglobin. The mutation that causes Tay-Sachs disease is located on the gene that codes for an enzyme called hexosaminidase A. For each of these recessive diseases, a person must inherit two copies of the mutated gene in order to have the disease.

As with Down syndrome, some disorders are caused by chromosome abnormalities. Girls with Turner syndrome have one X sex chromosome but are missing all or part of the other X chromosome. A specially trained geneticist can look at a karyotype to see if there are any chromosome abnormalities. Although scientists can identify the abnormality behind a disorder, they are still working to understand what causes these abnormalities and how to prevent them.

CHROMOSOME ABNORMALITY

Sometimes, there is a change in the number or the arrangement of chromosomes. Changes or damage to DNA and chromosomes can occur either before or after a baby is born. Chromosome abnormalities come in the form of deletions, duplications, translocations, and inversions.

• A deletion occurs when a piece of chromosome, along with the genetic information that was on that chromosome, is missing.

• Other times, a piece of a chromosome is duplicated and too much DNA is present.

• When a translocation occurs, a piece of a chromosome has broken off and attached to another chromosome, which may affect gene expression.

• An inversion occurs when a section of DNA is deleted and then reinserted in a reversed position, which may affect how the gene is expressed.

• A person may even have an entire extra copy of a chromosome (trisomy) or may be missing one entire chromosome (monosomy).

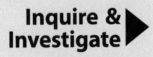

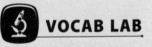
VOCAB LAB

Write down what you think each word means: **mutation, adaptation, mutagens, translocation, somatic mutation, trisomy,** and **monosomy.** Discuss your definitions with friends. Did you all come up with the same definitions? Turn to the text and the glossary if you need help.

SKIN COLOR IN DIFFERENT GEOGRAPHIC POPULATIONS

Have you ever wondered why people from different parts of the world have different colored skin? Why do people from the tropics generally have darker skin color that those who live in colder climates? Sometimes, variations in an organism are the result of mutations that occurred over time to help the organism adapt to its environment. How would you use genetics to explain skin color variations?

- **Skin color is a genetic trait that is passed from parent to child.** The genes for skin color have adapted or mutated over time. Some people have light-colored skin, while others have dark-colored skin. Why do you think this mutation occurred? Think about what causes skin color variations in areas close to the equator, areas closer to the poles, and coastal regions. In developing your hypothesis, consider the following facts:

  a. Melanin, the skin's brown pigment, is a natural sunscreen.

  b. A certain amount of UV rays helps the human body use vitamin D to absorb the calcium necessary for strong bones.

  c. Coastal peoples eat diets rich in seafood, which is an alternate source of vitamin D.

- **After you have developed your hypothesis to explain why skin color varies by geographic region, read the following page, "Human Skin Color Variation," at the Smithsonian National Museum of Natural History.** How does your hypothesis compare to what you read?

To investigate more, think about what other genetic variations could be the result of a favorable gene mutation. Develop a hypothesis to explain the variation. Research online and compare the information you find with your hypothesis.

AH HA! SO THAT IS WHY I SUNBURN SO EASILY...WHAT ELSE CAN I FIGURE OUT?

>DNA< Mutations can occur when DNA is being copied or when environmental factors such as ultraviolet light or radiation damage DNA.

GENE MUTATIONS

Gene mutations can be devastating. A single error in a nucleotide base can cause a critical protein to malfunction or not work at all. Other times, a gene mutation has little effect on an organism. In this activity, you will design a three-letter coded message that contains a gene mutation that does not significantly alter the message.

- **Create a sentence that uses only three-letter words.** Use your imagination to write something fun.

- **Are there ways to create mutations in your sentence?** Can you use each of these—an insertion, deletion, or incorrect letter—that does not significantly change the message?

- **Is there a mutation that might change the meaning of the sentence but still create a meaningful message?**

To investigate more, see how many changes you can make before the message becomes unreadable.

Chapter 8 ▶
Genetic Advances

MAYBE SOMEDAY GENE THERAPY COULD END VISION PROBLEMS!

How can scientists use genetics to improve our lives?

Genetics has helped scientists treat diseases and improve food sources, but these researchers must work with an eye to unintended consequences of their discoveries.

Every day, scientists learn more about genes and how they work. This knowledge has led to many scientific advances and medical breakthroughs. Scientists are using genetics not just to treat disease, but in unexpected ways as well, such as catching criminals and improving food crops. Do you have a friend with a Goldendoodle or a Yorkipoo? Genetics made these breeds of designer dog possible.

Yet even as science advances, many people are concerned that scientists may be reaching too far. Could they interfere too much with natural processes that may be better left untouched?

DNA FINGERPRINTING

Today, forensic scientists use DNA to solve crimes. Using blood, hair, and other body substances found at a crime scene, forensic experts help identify a suspect or a victim.

FINGERPRINTS

Every cell in your body holds DNA. The order of the bases and DNA sequence for every person, animal, and plant is unique. Remember, if you're not an identical twin, no one else has the same DNA as you. Investigators can compare DNA found at a crime scene to DNA from a suspect. If it matches, the investigator has linked the suspect to the crime scene.

It's fascinating what forensic scientists can do with even the smallest pieces of trace evidence. After using their expertise to collect DNA crime scene samples, they bring the samples to a lab without contaminating the evidence. At the lab, scientists can extract the DNA from the sample.

Once the DNA has been isolated, they cut it into fragments of different lengths. They separate the fragments using a process called gel electrophoresis, which separates fragments of molecules by size. DNA samples are loaded into a gel and placed into an electrophoresis chamber. In the chamber, a small electric current is passed through the gel, creating a negative pole and a positive pole in the gel. Because phosphate always carries a negative charge and it is part of the makeup of the sides of a DNA ladder, DNA carries a negative charge.

During electrophoresis, the DNA moves toward the positive pole carrying an opposite charge. Smaller fragments move more quickly than larger fragments, allowing scientists to separate them for further analysis and create a DNA fingerprint.

Investigators use fingerprints to identify a suspect. Because no two people have the same prints, investigators can link suspects to crime scenes if they can match fingerprints. As genetic science has advanced, criminal agencies can also use DNA to identify suspects. DNA is like a fingerprint that is unique to each individual. Investigators can use DNA at a crime scene to identify a suspect.

DID YOU KNOW?

The first cases to use DNA fingerprinting as evidence appeared in the courts in 1986. You can watch this video to learn more about the process of DNA fingerprinting and DNA profiling and how they are used in forensics and paternity cases.

FOR EXAMPLE, DNA CAN BE USED TO DETERMINE IF SOMEONE WAS AT A CRIME... ALL INVESTIGATORS NEED ARE HAIR OR SKIN CELLS!

THE DNA EVIDENCE CAN ALSO HELP PROVE SOMEONE'S INNOCENCE IN A COURT OF LAW!

Several factors affect DNA at a crime scene. Heat, sunlight, moisture, bacteria, and mold can damage a DNA sample. Therefore, not all DNA evidence will be useful in an investigation. If it is too damaged, scientists may not be able to use the sample as a match against a suspect's DNA.

In addition, DNA found at a crime scene does not have a time stamp. While investigators may be able to link a suspect to the scene through DNA, they usually cannot use it to determine when the suspect was there or how long he or she spent at the scene.

GENETIC DISEASE TESTING

As the understanding of genes has increased, scientists have also begun to understand the role of genes in devastating diseases. Many people carry alleles that cause genetic disease without ever realizing it. Single-gene diseases only show up when someone inherits two defective genes, one from each parent. Otherwise, that person will not have the disease, but is a carrier and could pass the defective gene to his or her children.

Genetic testing emerged when doctors realized that some fatal illnesses were more common in certain families and ethnic groups. Testing these patients helped doctors identify the disease-causing genes. Today, genetic testing in adults is used to diagnose disease or identify a patient as a carrier of a genetic disease. Doctors also use genetic testing to assess a person's risk of contracting certain diseases.

Today, there are gene tests for more than 1,300 diseases, with many more in development. To conduct a genetic test, doctors examine and sequence DNA from a blood or skin sample to determine if there are any gene mutations.

While early tests focused on single-gene diseases such as cystic fibrosis and hemophilia, more advanced genetic screening studies are in development to link more complex diseases with multiple genes and factors such as type 2 diabetes, Alzheimer's, and heart disease.

In addition to testing adults, genetic testing can also be performed before a child is born. Doctors can either genetically test embryos conceived through in vitro fertilization before they are implanted in the mother's uterus, or the fetus can be tested while in the womb. This testing can screen for chromosome abnormalities such as Down syndrome and genetic diseases such as cystic fibrosis.

GENE THERAPY

Beyond genetic testing for diagnosis, scientists are working to use their knowledge of genes to design new ways to treat, prevent, and cure disease. Gene therapy is an approach that attempts to fix genetic diseases at their source, by replacing the defective gene with a corrected copy of the gene. Scientists hope that this type of treatment will allow cells, tissues, and organs affected by the defective gene to function properly.

Although the idea of gene therapy sounds simple, it is actually quite complex. One of the biggest challenges in gene therapy research is figuring out how to deliver the corrected gene to a patient's DNA. The delivery has to target the right cells, enter the cell's nucleus, and be turned on so that the protein it produces does its job. In addition, the added gene must stay in place and keep working as part of the patient's DNA. Finally, the process cannot cause any harmful side effects to the patient. If the body sees the added gene as a toxin, it may trigger an immune response that attacks the gene and its delivery vehicle.

Ⅳ Most genetic tests can be performed with a blood sample. Occasionally, other tissues are used for testing.

DID YOU KNOW?

Although many scientists around the world have studied gene therapies to treat and prevent disease, no gene therapies have been approved for use in the United States to date. You can watch this video to learn more about what gene therapy is and how scientists can use it to change your genetic code.

🧬 There is an ex vivo approach to deliver genes. It involves removing the target cells from the body, delivering the gene to the cell outside the body, and then reinserting the cells into the body.

FLAVR SAVR TOMATO

The first commercially grown, genetically engineered food to hit store shelves was the Flavr Savr tomato. Approved by the FDA in 1994, the Flavr Savr had a gene inserted that slowed the tomato's natural ripening process. This gene prevented softening and rotting, which allowed the tomato to stay fresh longer. The Flavr Savr did not last long in stores, however. Because the tomatoes were delicate, they were difficult to transport. Also, many people did not like the tomato's bland taste. By 1997, the genetically modified tomatoes were no longer produced.

To insert genes, scientists need an effective delivery vehicle, called a vector. Some possible vectors that scientists are researching include several types of viruses. To deliver genes into a patient's body, doctors can inject a vector carrying the new gene into the body and target affected cells, a process called an in vivo approach.

Gene therapy is a great challenge in modern medicine and has had only limited success so far. Even so, researchers around the world continue to work to find a way to use gene therapy to treat and cure genetic disease.

GENETIC MODIFICATION

One of the most controversial ways genetic technology is being used is in the creation of genetically modified plants and animals. Genetic modification takes genes from other plants or animals and inserts them into a target plant or animal. Genetic modification can be done with plants, animals, or microorganisms.

Throughout history, farmers and breeders have used selective breeding to create crops and offspring that have desired traits. They chose to mate or cross individual animals or plants that carried the gene for a desired characteristic in the hope that the offspring would too. Sweet corn, seedless watermelon, and purebred dogs are examples of living things that have been enhanced by selective breeding.

With genetic engineering, scientists can speed up the process of producing offspring with desirable traits. Instead of breeding or crossing two parents, scientists simply move the desired genes from one plant to another, or between an animal and a plant. Genetic engineering is a way for farmers to grow larger, better-quality crops in less time, with less effort, and for less money.

What are some of the other benefits of genetic engineering? Food that is more nutritious and tastes better. Genetically engineered crops can produce plants that grow faster, are more disease- and drought-resistant and need less pesticide. Genetic engineering can also help the growth of foods that could be used for vaccines or medicines.

As every gardener knows, beetles can quickly ruin a lovely tomato plant. Some genetically modified tomato plants, however, are resistant to beetles. To create this plant, scientists transferred genes from a bacterium into the tomato plant's genome. The gene codes for a protein that is poisonous to certain insects, including the beetle. The resulting tomato plant produces a natural pesticide, which now makes it resistant to the beetle. The plant's future offspring will inherit the gene, making future generations also beetle-resistant.

CLONING

Scientists can clone an organism by creating an exact genetic copy of it. Every piece of DNA is identical between the original and the clone. Some scientists believe that cloning may be an important tool to saving endangered animals and growing cells, tissues, and organs for people who need transplants.

How does cloning work? In 2003, scientists cloned an African wildcat at the Audubon Center for Research of Endangered Species in New Orleans, Louisiana. They removed an egg cell from a female house cat. Then scientists removed the cat's DNA from the egg's nucleus and inserted DNA from Jazz, an African wildcat. They applied a small amount of electricity to the egg, so it would divide and grow into an embryo. Next, the scientists reinserted the egg in the female house cat, who became pregnant. The resulting kitten, named Ditteaux, was the exact DNA clone of Jazz.

CORN, FOR EXAMPLE, IS ONE OF THE MOST WIDELY PRODUCED GMO'S.

GENETICALLY MODIFIED ORGANISMS OR GMO'S, ARE A HOT-BUTTON ISSUE NOWADAYS.

In the United States, many crops are genetically modified. Corn, papayas, soybeans are all examples of crops that have been genetically modified. Most people eat them every day in pizza, bread, cereal, or ice cream.

Genetic modification takes genes from other plants or animals and inserts them into a target plant or animal. Cloning creates an exact genetic copy of an organism. Every piece of DNA is identical between the original and the clone.

How do scientists hope to use cloning? Scientists think that cloning for medical purposes will one day help a large number of people. Scientists are researching ways to use cloned embryos to grow human cells. Embryos contain special cells called embryonic stem cells. Because these cells do not yet have a specific job, they have the ability to transform into any type of cell in the body. An embryonic stem cell could grow into a heart, blood, skin, or many other types of cells. Scientists hope that one day they will be able to use stems cells to help sick and injured people replace damaged tissue or organs.

Scientists may also one day use cloning to study disease. Researchers often use animals such as mice to learn about human disease. Cloning would enable scientists to create genetically identical animals for study in a short period. Currently, animals such as cows, sheep, and goats are genetically engineered to create drugs or proteins that are needed for medicines. Cloning may be a faster way to create the large quantities of genetically engineered animals needed for medicines.

Some people wonder if cloning may one day be a way to bring back extinct plant and animal species. In the movie *Jurassic Park*, scientists use dinosaur DNA that had been preserved for millions of years to clone dinosaurs. In theory, it would be possible to clone an extinct species if scientists had a well-preserved source of DNA from the extinct organism and a closely related species that could serve as a surrogate mother.

Scientists have already attempted to clone an endangered animal. They cloned a gaur, a rare, ox-like animal from Southeast Asia. They used a cow as a surrogate mother to carry the cloned gaur. The cloned gaur was born successfully and named Noah. Two days after birth, however, it died from a bacterial infection. Cloning a long-extinct animal such as the woolly mammoth would be much more difficult, however, because the scientists have not found a well-preserved source of DNA.

ISSUES

Although the idea of cloning may be exciting, successful cloning is not easy. To date, scientists have experienced a high failure rate when attempting to clone animals. For every 1,000 cloning attempts, only between one and 30 are successful, or 0.1 to 3 percent. Many factors can lead to failure, including incompatibility between the egg and transferred nucleus, the egg not developing properly, failure of the embryo's implantation, or the pregnancy itself. In some cases, problems occur in later development. Cloned animals may be bigger at birth, which can lead to breathing and blood-flow problems.

In addition, many people are concerned that cloning animals may lead one day to cloning a human being. Some people believe that human cloning could be used to help infertile couples have children or to replace a child who died. Others, however, believe that cloning humans interferes with natural human life cycles and presents many ethical, legal, and social issues.

GROWING A LIVER

Scientists hope that one day stem cells will be able to grow new organs to transplant into waiting patients. In 2013, stem cell biologists in Japan came one step closer to that goal. Researchers at the Yokohama City University mixed three cell types—adult stem cells engineered for a human liver, adult bone marrow stem cells, and human umbilical cord stem cells. In a petri dish, the cells combined and formed a tiny liver bud. The bud is a three-dimensional piece of liver that contains a system to deliver blood to the organ. The scientists successfully transplanted the liver bud into a mouse, where the transplanted liver brought the mouse back from liver failure. The scientists concluded that the liver bud was functioning like a human liver.

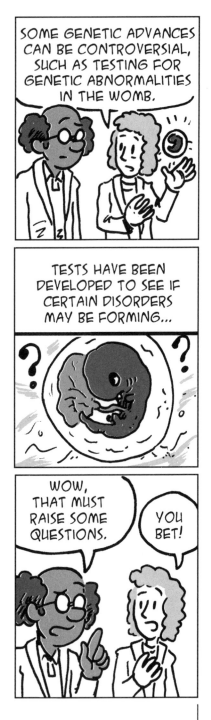

GENETIC MARKERS: FOLLOWING THE DNA TRAIL

When DNA passes from one generation to the next, it combines in ways that make each offspring unique. At the same time, some parts of the DNA chain are passed mostly intact from generation to generation. Occasionally, these intact sections are changed by mutations, which create genetic markers. Scientists can trace the passage of genetic markers from generation to generation. By tracing genetic markers through time, scientists can identify a common ancestor for everyone who carries a particular marker.

Scientists with National Geographic are using genetic markers to chart ancient human migrations from Africa across the continents. Launched in 2005, the Genographic Project uses advanced DNA analysis to track and map genetic markers in people today. With this information, they are creating a picture of when and where ancient humans moved around the globe. You can visit this website to learn more about the Genographic Project.

ETHICAL QUESTIONS

Many people are concerned about the way the genetic advances and technology are being used now and may be used in the future. As research pushes the limits of what genetics can do, debates arise. When does human intervention into the basic code of life go too far?

For many people, changing the genetic code of future generations is morally wrong and too risky. Millions of genes interact with each other in ways that are not yet fully known. Changing the DNA code may trigger unexpected side effects in future generations with no way to reverse the damage.

Opponents of genetically modified food worry that changing the DNA of crops will affect the environment in negative ways. Pollen from insect-killing crops could kill other wildlife. It could also be absorbed by weeds, creating insect-resistant plants that take over an ecosystem. Others are concerned that genetically modified foods may contain allergens that trigger serious allergic reactions.

On the other hand, it's been proven that scientists might be able to remove or inhibit the proteins that act as allergens for some people. Give it some thought. It's an interesting debate. The genetically modified sweet-tasting Bt-corn has an insect-killing gene. No spraying means less harm to the environment and the workers handling the toxic spray. But the same gene also appears to kill the monarch butterfly. Also, a large percentage of animal feed is made up of genetically modified soybeans that can make their way into your body. So how do you know that you are not eating genetically modified food? The only way to know for sure is to buy organic products.

Many people also believe that it is morally wrong to experiment on embryonic stem cells. The process destroys the embryo, which they believe takes a life.

As genetics research advances, ethical questions will continue. New techniques and therapies that are not known today will lead to new questions tomorrow. With each discovery, researchers will carefully try to balance science and ethics.

AND IT'LL BE UP TO THE NEXT GENERATION TO CONTINUE TO ASK THOSE QUESTIONS AND DO GOOD RESEARCH.

Critics of genetic testing fear that it might someday become a tool to build a designer baby. Genetic tests can already help parents using in vitro fertilization to select a boy or girl embryo to implant. In the future, pre-implantation tests may allow parents to select other characteristics for their baby, such as height, hair color, and intelligence.

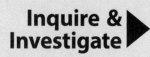
CREATE YOUR OWN GMO

Scientists have used genetic engineering to create species of plants and animals that have desired traits. In the popular novel The Hunger Games, *there are a variety of genetically modified organisms, from jabberjays to tracker jackers. Often these creatures are designed for a specific purpose, but later act in unexpected ways. In the case of* The Hunger Games' *jabberjay, the genetically modified bird was designed to spy, but unexpectedly mated with another species of bird to create a brand new species called the mockingjay. This result was an unintended and unforeseen consequence of the government's decision to create the jabberjay in the first place.*

In this project, you will design your own genetically modified organism. You may design an organism that could be used by government, schools, or yourself. Then you will think about the effects your organism may have, intended and unintended.

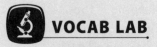

VOCAB LAB

Write down what you think each word means: **forensic scientist, gel electrophoresis, in vitro fertilization, gene therapy, vector, in vivo, genetic modification, embryonic stem cells**, and **cloning**. Discuss your definitions with friends. Did you all come up with the same definitions? Turn to the text and the glossary if you need help.

- **Decide what type of genetically modified organism you would like to create.** For inspiration you may want to research ideas and organisms on the Internet.

- **Once you have decided what type of genetically modified organism you would create, consider and document the following:**

  a. What traits will the organism have? Why did you design it? What need does it fill?

  b. Will it be used by government, schools, or individuals? How will it be used?

- **Create an illustration or prototype of your organism.** Present information about its origins and special characteristics.

- **Think about what drawbacks or problems could arise because of the new organism.** What are the benefits? Will the problems and complications hurt others? If so, how? What other risks exist because of your organism?

- **Do you think the benefits outweigh the risks for your genetically modified organism?** Why or why not?

> To investigate more, take the position of a group that opposes your new creation. Develop an argument against creating the genetically modified organism. What opposition points are the most convincing?`

Ideas for Supplies ▼

- several different commercial bar codes with the numbers cut off
- 2 commercial bar codes that are identical (from the same product) with the numbers cut off
- paper and pencil
- tape
- hand magnifiers
- ink pad
- damp paper towels

THROUGH THE POWER OF DNA I WILL FIND OUT WHO MADE THE MESS.

USE DNA TO SOLVE A CRIME

If you were a forensic scientist investigating a robbery, you might ask crime scene investigators at the scene of the crime to collect a blood sample that they believed came from a guilty person. They would also collect DNA samples from each suspect. It is your job to examine each of the samples and determine if you can match the DNA from the crime scene to one of the suspects. Can you catch the crook?

- **Tape each of the bar codes to a piece of paper so that you can see them easily.** Label one of the two identical bar codes "Blood DNA at Crime Scene." Label all the others in a way that will help you keep track of each one. These represent DNA samples from suspects of the crime.

- **Shuffle the remaining bar codes.** Can you examine each of the suspect's DNA and compare it to the DNA from the crime scene? What are looking for?

- **Does one of the suspects match the crime scene DNA?** Which one? Explain how you made the match. What can you conclude from your findings?

To investigate more, set up a scenario where none of the suspect samples match the crime scene sample. What can you conclude from your findings? What recommendation would you give investigators? What if you tried to make a match with only half of the crime scene DNA available? Would you still have enough information to link a suspect to the scene?

abnormality: a difference from what is normal, usually in a negative way.

adaptation: a mutation that is beneficial to an organism.

allele: one of the forms of a gene.

amino acid: a molecule made of hydrogen, oxygen, carbon, and nitrogen atoms that links with other amino acids to form a protein chain.

anticodon: three adjacent nucleotide bases in transfer RNA that bind to a corresponding codon in messenger RNA. Designates a specific amino acid during the building of a protein.

atom: the smallest particle of matter.

autosomal: a chromosome that is not a sex chromosome.

biological: relating to life and living processes.

biology: the science of life and living organisms.

blend: to mix different varieties.

breeding: the development of new types of plants and animals with improved characteristics.

carrier: an organism that has the gene for a trait that is not expressed in his or her system.

cell: the most basic part of a living thing. Billions of cells make up a plant or animal.

centromere: a point on a chromosome that appears during cell division where sister chromatids are joined.

characteristic: a feature of a person, such as blue eyes or curly hair.

chemistry: the science of the properties of substances and how substances react with one another.

chloroplasts: structures in plant cells that convert the sun's energy into sugars.

chromatid: each of the two threadlike strands into which a chromosome divides longitudinally during cell division.

chromatin: a mass of genetic material made of DNA and proteins that condense to form chromosomes during eukaryotic cell division.

chromosome: the part of a cell that contains genes.

clone: an exact genetic copy.

co-dominance: when both alleles of a trait are expressed, for example, AB blood type.

codon: a combination of three nucleotides in an mRNA that translates to an amino acid.

crop: a plant grown for food and other uses.

crossing over: the exchange of segments between homologous chromosomes that happens during meiosis and contributes to genetic variation.

cytokinesis: the division of a cell following replication and division of its chromosomes.

cytoplasm: the jelly-like fluid inside a cell.

deletion: a mutation that occurs when a part of a chromosome or a sequence of DNA is missing.

diploid: having two copies of each chromosome.

DNA: the substance that carries your genetic information, the "blueprint" of who you are. It is the abbreviation for deoxyribonucleic acid.

dominant: a genetic trait that hides the expression of a recessive trait.

duplication: a chromosome abnormality where a piece of chromosome is duplicated.

embryonic stem cell: a cell within an embryo that has not yet been assigned a specific job.

enzyme: a protein that speeds up a chemical reaction in a living organism.

ethical: acting in a way that upholds someone's belief in right and wrong.

ethnic group: people of the same race or nationality who share a distinctive culture.

eukaryote: an organism, such as an animal, made up of cells that have a membrane-bound nucleus with genetic material organized into chromosomes.

evolution: the theory of how species develop from earlier forms of life. Natural variation in the genetic material of a population favors reproduction by some individuals more than others, so that over the generations all members of the population come to possess the favorable traits.

ex vivo: taking place outside an organism.

F1 generation: the offspring of a cross between two individuals of the parental generation.

F2 generation: the offspring of a cross between two individuals of the F1 generation.

fertilize: to join female and male cells to produce seeds and offspring.

forensic scientist: an expert who analyzes and explains evidence found at a crime scene using chemical and physical analysis.

foundation: the basis on which something is supported or built.

frameshift mutation: a mutation in a DNA chain that occurs when the number of nucleotides inserted or deleted is not a multiple of three.

fundamental: something that is of central importance.

gamete: a male or female cell involved in reproduction.

gel electrophoresis: a process that separates fragments of molecules by size using an electric current.

gene: a section of DNA that codes for a particular trait.

gene expression: the process by which information in a gene is used to produce a protein or other gene product.

generation: a group born and living at about the same time.

gene therapy: a treatment that replaces a defective gene with a corrected copy of the gene.

genetic disorder: a disease or condition that results from an inability of a gene or genes to function normally.

genetic modification: taking genes from plants or animals and inserting them into a target plant or animal.

genetics: the study of genes and heredity.

genome: an organism's full set of chromosomes.

genotype: the genes of an organism.

germline mutation: an error that occurs during meiosis in producing an egg or sperm cell.

glucose: a basic sugar that provides energy.

GMOS: genetically modified organisms, or organisms whose DNA has been altered using genetic engineering.

haploid: having one copy of each chromosome.

helix: something spiral in form.

heredity: the passing of traits from parents to offspring.

heterozygous: having two different alleles for a gene.

histone: a protein that helps DNA coil into compact units.

homologous: chromosome pairs, one from each parent, that are similar in length, gene position, and centromere location.

homozygous: having two of the same alleles for a gene.

hormone: a messenger that tells certain cells in different parts of your body what to do.

Human Genome Project: an effort by scientists worldwide to identify and map all of the human genome's 3 billion base pairs.

hybrid: the offspring of two animals or plants of different species or varieties.

hydrogen bond: a weak chemical bond between atoms, similar to the attraction of opposite magnetic poles, that occurs across short distances and is easily formed and broken.

hypothesis: a prediction or unproven idea that tries to explain certain facts or observations. Plural is *hypotheses*.

incomplete dominance: when an organism has alleles for different traits but neither trait is dominant over the other.

inheritance: passing characteristics from parents to offspring.

inherited: passed down from parents.

insertion: a mutation that occurs when an extra nucleotide is inserted into the DNA chain.

interphase: a period of cell growth between divisions when the cell grows and functions normally.

inversion: an abnormality where a section of DNA is deleted and reinserted in a reversed position.

in vitro fertilization: the process of joining a woman's egg and a man's sperm outside the body in a laboratory.

in vivo: taking place inside a living organism.

karyotype: a picture of an organism's chromosomes, lined up by shape and size.

law of independent assortment: the idea that allele pairs separate independently when gametes are formed so that traits are passed to offspring independently of other traits.

law of segregation: the idea that alleles for a trait separate randomly when gametes are formed.

macromolecule: a large molecule, usually made of at least 100 atoms.

maggot: the worm-shaped larva of various members of the fly family, found in rotting matter.

meiosis: cell division in sexually reproducing organisms that reduces the amount of genetic information by half.

membrane: a thin covering.

mitochondria: organelles within a cell that convert glucose into energy.

mitosis: the process of cell division.

molecular biologist: a scientist who studies the structure of the molecules of living things.

monastery: a house for people, such as monks, who have taken religious vows.

monk: a man who lives in a religious community and devotes himself to prayer.

monosomy: a chromosome abnormality where a person is missing a copy of a chromosome.

mutagens: environmental agents that damage DNA.

mutation: a permanent change in a gene.

nitrogen base: an organic compound containing nitrogen—adenine, guanine, cytosine, and thymine make up the rungs of the ladder in DNA.

GLOSSARY

nuclear pore: a space for RNA and proteins to pass through the nuclear membrane.

nucleosome: the repeating subunits of chromatin, consisting of a DNA chain coiled around a core of histones.

nucleotide: a basic unit of DNA made of a sugar joined to a nitrogen base on one side and to a phosphate group on the other side.

nucleus: the part of a cell that controls how it functions.

offspring: a child of two parents.

organelle: a structure within a cell that has a special function.

organic compound: a group of two or more atoms bound together. It includes carbon and hydrogen and may also contain other elements.

organism: any living thing, such as a plant or animal.

oxygen: a gas in the air that people and animals need to breathe to stay alive and which is the most plentiful element on the earth.

P1 generation: the first set of parents to be crossed.

pedigree: a chart that can show the phenotypes of individuals in a family to highlight how a trait is inherited.

phenotype: the way an organism looks.

phosphate group: a phosphate atom bound to four oxygen atoms.

pistil: the female, seed-producing reproductive part of a flower. It includes the ovary, style, and stigma.

point mutation: a mutation that occurs when the wrong nucleotide is placed in a DNA sequence.

pollen: a fine, yellow powder produced by flowering plants. Pollen fertilizes the seeds of other plants as it gets spread around by the wind, birds, and insects.

pollination: transferring male pollen to the female stigma.

predisposition: a tendency to have a particular condition.

probability: how likely something is to happen.

prokaryote: an organism, such as bacteria, made up of cells without a nucleus or any membrane-bound organelles.

promoter: a region of DNA that identifies where a gene starts.

proofreading: the ability of DNA to find and correct mistakes when replicating.

protein: a group of large molecules composed of chains of amino acids. Proteins are an essential part of all living things.

Punnett square: a diagram that is used to predict an outcome of a genetic cross or breeding experiment.

recessive: a genetic trait that is hidden when a dominant trait is present.

replication: process of making an exact copy of a DNA molecule.

reproduction: making something new, just like itself.

resemblance: the state of looking like or acting like someone or something else.

respiration: breathing.

ribosome: the protein-making factory in the cell.

RNA polymerase: the enzyme that synthesizes RNA from a DNA template during transcription.

RNA: ribonucleic acid, the molecule that transfers information carried by DNA to the protein factories in the cell.

scientific method: a set of techniques for learning something new or investigating a problem.

self-pollinate: when a plant's pollen falls onto its own stigma.

sequence: the order of things.

sex-linked trait: a trait that is controlled by genes on one of the sex chromosomes.

sister chromatids: identical copies of chromosomes that are linked by a centromere.

somatic mutation: an error that occurs during mitosis, after conception, and during life.

species: a group of living things that are closely related and look like each other.

spindle: a structure in the cell that organizes and separates chromosomes during cell division.

spontaneous: something that happens by itself without an apparent cause.

stamen: the male, pollen-producing reproductive part of a flower. It includes the filament and anther.

stable: firmly established and not likely to change.

stigma: the upper part of the pistil, which receives pollen.

stimulus: a change in an organism's environment that causes an action, activity, or response. Plural is *stimuli*.

telomere: the tip of a chromosome.

terminator: a region of DNA that signals the end of a gene.

tetrad: a paired set of homologous chromosomes, each composed of two sister chromatids, that forms during the first phase of meiosis.

tissue: a group or mass of similar cells working together to perform common functions.

trace evidence: small but measurable items such as fibers, skin cells, powders, or soil.

trait: a feature or quality that makes somebody or something recognizable.

transcription factor: a protein that binds to specific DNA sequences.

transcription: the process in which DNA is used to make a strand of messenger RNA.

translation: the process in which messenger RNA attaches to a ribosome and creates a protein.

translocation: an abnormality where a piece of chromosome has broken off and attached to another chromosome.

trisomy: a chromosome abnormality where a person has an extra copy of a chromosome.

Universal Genetic Code: the sequence of nucleotides in DNA or RNA that determines the specific amino acid sequence when building proteins.

variation: a different form of something.

vector: a delivery vehicle such as a virus used to insert genes in gene therapy.

virus: a small infectious agent that can replicate only inside the living cells of an organism.

widow's peak: a v-shaped point in the hairline in the center of the forehead.

zygote: a fertilized egg resulting from the joining of a sperm and egg cell.

▾ RESOURCES

↪ BOOKS

Cell Division and Genetics
Robert Snedden, Heinemann-Raintree, 2007.

DNA and Blood: Dead People Do Tell Tales
Sara L. Latta, Enslow, 2011.

Double Helix: The Quest to Uncover the Structure of DNA
Glen Phelan, National Geographic, 2006.

Genetics: A Living Blueprint
Darlene R. Stille, Compass Point Books, 2006.

Genetic Engineering
Marina Cohen, Crabtree, 2009.

Genetics for Dummies
Tara Rodden Robinson, Wiley, 2010.

Genetics: From DNA to Designer Dogs
Kathleen Simpson, National Geographic, 2008.

Genetics: Investigating the Function of Genes and the Science of Heredity
Trevor Day, Rosen, 2012.

↪ GENETIC EXPERIMENTS

Genetics and Evolution: Science Fair Projects
Robert Gardner, Enslow, 2010.

Genetics Experiments
Pamela Walker and Elaine Wood, Facts on File, 2010.

Projects in Genetics
Claire O'Neal, Mitchell Lane, 2010.

↪WEBSITES

American Museum of Natural History
The museum's "Gene Scene" page has kid-friendly information and activities about genetics.
http://www.amnh.org/explore/ology/genetics

DNA
Visit this site to learn more about DNA and how it can be used to identify a suspect.
http://scienceforkids.kidipede.com/biology/cells/dna.htm

Dynamic Timeline
This website from the National Human Genome Research Institute has an informative timeline that details important events in genetics history.
http://www.genome.gov/25019887

Learn Genetics
This website features articles, interactive modules, and activities to study genetics.
http://learn.genetics.utah.edu/